Hawkins, Peter S.

The language of grace : Flannery O'Connor, Walker Percy & Iris Murdoch

THE LANGUAGE OF GRACE

International Standard Book No: 0-936384-07-7
Library of Congress Catalog No: 82-072130

Published in the United States of America
by Cowley Publications

printed by Shea Brothers, Inc.
cover design by James Madden, SSJE

THE LANGUAGE OF GRACE

Flannery O'Connor, Walker Percy,
&
Iris Murdoch

PETER S. HAWKINS

COWLEY

For Amelie Alice Hawkins
who is a great reader of books,
and for Thomas William Hawkins
who has always been sure I would write one.

PREFACE

Although books are usually written in solitude, and often at the expense of relationships, it is also true that they are inevitably the result of much informal collaboration, of time spent along beaches and on trains and in classrooms with other people. Certainly this book has developed in company. The idea for some study of O'Connor, Percy, and Murdoch came to me in 1977, as Barbara Mowat of Auburn University and I walked along the Gulf of Mexico fantasizing about books *someone* should write. What amounted to informal drafts were developed in a course in contemporary fiction at the Yale Divinity School, where my students' questions (and their enthusiasm) helped me focus my interests and substantiate my intuitions.

The invitation of the Society of St. John the Evangelist to deliver a series of lectures provided just enough pressure for these ideas to crystallize. The Society also afforded me a very live audience, at once challenging and receptive, so that the expanded version of those Cowley Lectures which eventually became *The Language of Grace* owes much to my interaction with that wonderful assembly of monks, Harvard students, and citizens of Cambridge. When the manuscript was completed, Barbara Mowat gave me the benefit of her fine editorial eye, so I have her to thank in the end as in the beginning.

Finally, throughout my involvement with the Cowley Fathers, from the Society's first overture to me until the publication of this book, Cynthia Logan has been an unfailing source of support, guidance, and fun—to use a playful word in this otherwise serious context. I am not sure how many authors discover a friend in their editors, but among the pleasures of writing this text has been that great joy.

Peter Hawkins
New Haven, 1982

CONTENTS

List of Abbreviations

CS Flannery O'Connor, *The Complete Stories* (New York: Farrar, Straus & Giroux, 1974).

L *The Habit of Being* (New York: Farrar, Straus & Giroux, 1979)

M *Mystery and Manners* (New York: Farrar, Straus & Giroux, 1979)

WB *Wise Blood* (New York: Farrar, Straus & Giroux, 1980)

LC Walker Percy, *Lancelot* (New York: Farrar, Straus & Giroux, 1977)

LG *The Last Gentleman* (New York: Farrar, Straus & Giroux, 1966)

LR *Love in the Ruins* (New York: Farrar, Straus & Giroux, 1971)

MB *The Message in the Bottle* (New York: Farrar, Straus & Giroux, 1975)

MG *The Moviegoer* (New York: Farrar, Straus & Giroux, 1967)

SC *The Second Coming* (New York: Farrar, Straus & Giroux, 1980)

AD Iris Murdoch, "Against Dryness," *Encounter* 16 (January 1961): 16-20.

B *The Bell* (London: Chatto & Windus, 1958).

EM "Existentialists and Mystics," in *Essays and Poems Presented to Lord David Cecil*, ed. W. W. Robson (London: Constable, 1970): 169-83.

FS *The Fire and the Sun: Why Plato Banished the Artists* (New York: Oxford University Press, 1977).

HC *Henry and Cato* (New York: Viking, 1976).

SG *The Sovereignty of Good* (New York: Schocken Books, 1971).

WC *A Word Child* (New York: Viking, 1975).

1 Strategies of Grace

In the first letter of what proved to be an extraordinary correspondence, Flannery O'Connor used the occasion of a "moronic" unsigned review to confide her frustrations with the contemporary audience for which she wrote: "It is easy to see that the moral sense has been bred out of certain sections of the population, like the wings have been bred off certain chickens to produce more white meat on them. This is the generation of wingless chickens, which I suppose is what Nietzsche meant when he said God was dead." In a less polemical letter to the same young woman, known to us only as "A," this moral sense which O'Connor found increasingly lacking in our time is spoken of as "the accurate naming of the things of God." The phrase is a gnomic one, but by it I take her to mean the whole theological frame of reference, concretely expressed in Scripture, that once provided the coherence for Western culture and imagination, but which does so no longer. O'Connor's occasionally ill-tempered frustration with this generation of wingless chickens grew out of an inability to assume (and thereby to share directly) this religious vision of reality with the reader. What she faced instead was a seemingly insurmountable problem of communication. How could she portray the transforming action of the divine within human life for people who no longer have a powerful sense of God, much less a world of symbols by which to understand and articulate religious experience? Deprived of the shared assumptions that allow direct address, O'Connor was bound by the need to find new modes of indirection, strategies of communication that might open the reader to dimensions of life become inaccessible to many and remote to most. In other words, she saw that she had to discover a new language of grace in order to confront the reader with the experience of God, for no matter how current His mysterious presence among us may be, O'Connor knew that the contemporary Christian writer had inherited a "coin of the realm which has the face worn off it" — what Walker Percy, using a similar metaphor, has called the *devaluation* of the old words of grace.[1]

What follows in this study is both an exploration of what this devaluation has meant to three mid-century authors and an analysis of their attempts in narrative to revitalize the religious imagination by putting the notion of grace, as it were, back into circulation. I have limited myself to fiction writers and, moreover, to those who have dealt openly and in nonfictional prose with contemporary problems of religious communication. For this reason Flannery O'Connor and Walker Percy come immediately to mind. Both are self-consciously Roman Catholic writers who feel themselves working somewhat in a vacuum, both have as their central preoccupation what O'Connor calls "the action of grace on a character not very willing to support it," and both have portrayed the drama that follows upon that action through the use of violence, comedy, the bizarre, and the grotesque.

My third choice, Iris Murdoch, may seem an odd addition to this company. Although she too is aware of the central loss of Christianity in Western culture, and perhaps all the more so from her vantage point in England, she is not herself a believer, but is rather in search of secular and moral equivalents for the discarded faith. While also preoccupied with conversion — the change of heart that becomes a change of life — she gives us in place of God as the end term her transcendent notion of the Good. As with O'Connor and Percy, there is in her fiction the reworking of a basic pattern of conversion: a person forced by extraordinary circumstances to transcend the self-centered demands of the ego, who comes to see another person as real and full and who can finally see that person without the distortions of fantasy or ulterior motive; who can, that is, love someone else. This formula sounds suspiciously like the one used again and again by Walker Percy, but in fact Murdoch's stories of conversion differ a great deal in their intended goal. For her it is entirely a matter of human beings responding *to* one another, rather than *through* one another to God. For her the transforming mystery of love into which her characters are called is the mystery of other persons.

We know O'Connor's withering perspective on all this from a letter written to a mutual friend about "A":

> I'll tell you what's with 'A,' why all the exhilaration. She has left the Church. Those are the signs of release. She's high as a kite and all on pure air. This conversion was achieved by Iris Murdoch. . . . [She] now sees through everything and loves everything and is a bundle of empathy for everything. She doesn't believe any longer that Christ is God and so she has found that he is 'beautiful, beautiful!' Everything is in the eeeek eeek eureka stage. The effect of all this on me is pretty sick-making but I manage to keep my mouth shut.
>
> (L 459-60)

The scorn heaped on Murdoch as a false prophet and bad influence is of a piece with O'Connor's general attitude toward the generation of wingless chickens for whom God is dead — or become the Good. And yet it seems to me to obscure an intriguing phenomenon in Murdoch's work: the ambiguity of interpretation occasioned by her extensive use of theological concepts and language. However exhausted or rejected the Christian tradition may be in the lives of her characters, its constant presence within the world of her novels raises the possibility that there is a divine reality independent of her own humanism. Something like the action of grace in O'Connor and Percy may also be found at work here, among the signs and wonders of her uncanny narratives. Murdoch offers us the possibility that a writer who uses the devalued words of grace may end up not only revaluing them, but also being used by them; that is, may end up writing fiction susceptible to a sacred, as well as a secular, reading. Everything depends on the interpretive choice of the reader.

It is with this latter point that we begin to see the more basic strategic differences in the kind of fiction under discussion here. If in O'Connor and Percy the reader is rhetorically led to infer from the text a Christian meaning — what O'Connor often referred to as the anagogical level — in Murdoch's work we are compelled only to choose how we will understand the narrative: the text is hermeneutically "open." Thus, we will not be asked to infer a single meaning even though it is often clear enough what the author herself is "thinking"; we will be asked instead to choose among options and to discover our own religious presuppositions in that choice.

Despite this wide divergence, what all three share is a concern with the mysterious life-transforming process of loss and discovery, of death and the possibility of rebirth, which we know as grace. They are writers who want to tell the story of transcendent experience in a period when people commonly lack the words to express it and therefore the means by which to enter it more deeply. They are writers, that is, who are working against the limits of contemporary imagination, both with and against the limitations of the reader.

It is by first looking at a kind of story-telling that flourished in the West for more than a millenium, however, that we can perhaps best appreciate the very different circumstances of our own time and the difficulties that now stand before any writer who sets out to explore an experience of grace. Let me offer for example the story of Caedmon, the first poet of the English language, which comes to us solely through the Venerable Bede's *Ecclesiastical History of the English People.* Tradition has it that Caedmon was a stable keeper at Whitby Abbey when Saint Hilda was abbess there in the seventh century. According to Bede, one night at a feast, as the harp was being passed around the abbey hall, Caedmon was so overcome with bashfulness that when the instrument was almost his — and with it the expectation of a song — he fled from the gathering and hid himself in a stable with the animals. That night he dreamed that someone came to him and said, "Caedmon, sing me something." He excused himself by saying that his inability to sing was the very reason he had fled from the hall. This was not compelling enough for the visitor, however, who once more asked him for a song, but this time with a specific theme: "the beginning of created things." Sing he did, but once he began there was no stopping, for the next morning as Bede continues, Caedmon

> sang of the creation of the world, the origin of the human race, and the whole of Genesis. He sang of Israel's departure from Egypt, of their entry into the land of promise, and many other events of scriptural history. He sang of the Lord's incarnation, passion, resurrection and ascension into heaven, the coming of the Holy Spirit, and the teaching of the apostles. He also made many poems on the terrors of the last judgment, the horrible pains of hell, and the joys of

> the kingdom of heaven. In addition to these he composed several other songs on the blessings and judgments of God, by which he sought to turn his hearers from delight in wickedness and to inspire them to love and do good.
>
> (4.24)

There are several things to take note of here, both with regard to Caedmon's spontaneous outpouring of sacred poetry and to Bede's account of it. In the first place, while Caedmon is asked to tell only the tale of page one, "the beginning of created things," he is forced by the sheer coherence of the story to tell it all the way through, from Creation through Apocalypse. This is because his consciousness is essentially biblical and the Bible, as it is shaped by canon, knows its end in the beginning and its beginning in the end. Within its covers is a vision of all reality embraced, where, as Dante says of what he sees at the end of *Paradiso,* all is "bound by love in one volume" (33.86). For this reason the particular events of history are given a universal context, a framework in which to be understood and evaluated, whether they be the actions of the first human parents, or of Israel, or of the Church, or of any individual at any given "now." The paradox here is that while in one sense the Bible is a very closed book, to which nothing may be added and nothing taken away, it is continuously opening itself up to the contemporary reality of the believer, "evangelizing" human experience by making each isolated moment or event meaningful in terms of its whole.

This brings me to my second observation, which is that Bede's story of Caedmon is itself "biblical" in its narration and the bashful poet a type familiar in Scripture. For Caedmon in his shyness running away from the crowded hall, Caedmon declining an angelic visitor's command to sing, Caedmon dreaming himself a poet and then, *mirabile dictu*, that dream coming true: what is this but a version of Moses stammering before Yahweh about being "slow of speech and of tongue"? Or Isaiah claiming unclean lips, and Jeremiah his youth and inexperience, as sufficient reason for saying no to God's call? Or the terrified disciples provoking Jesus to tell them not to take thought for what they would say in public — because clearly there was nothing they wanted to do more than disappear to some stable and fall asleep, close-mouthed, in the hay? Whatever the personal peculiarities of Caedmon may have been, whatever the uniqueness of his experience, Bede presents him as a type in a tradition that runs throughout the Old Testament and the New. He is the one who is reluctant to speak, but who cannot in the end reject the words placed in his mouth; the one who confesses with Jeremiah, "If I say, 'I will not mention him, or speak anymore in his name,' there is in my heart as it were a burning fire shut up in my bones, and I am weary holding it in, and I cannot."

What we see here is the power of the Bible to incorporate other stories into its larger and ongoing narrative. Thus Caedmon himself, no less than his hymn about the beginning of created things, can be seen as a paraphrase of Scripture. His life thus gains not only in intelligibility, but in resonance: he means something more than himself. What is more, if Bede's Caedmon gains by being incorporated into the context of Scripture, so too does he enrich it by his personal reenactment of it, by re-presenting its typology in his own time and place. For Bede sees that it is not only on Mt. Horeb, from out of the burning bush, that God confronts the one who is afraid to speak, but also in the stable of a place like Whitby, among real cows. In this same way the painters of the German Middle Ages portrayed Christ's nativity in snow, with wise men that look like hearty northern princes and the Virgin a blonde *Hausfrau*. This is not, I think, a case of simple anachronism;

it is, rather, a bold appropriation of the ancient story for the here and now in which the believer lives.

Aside from the universal scope of Caedmon's song and the typology of Bede's account, what remains to be noted is the end, or goal, of both the poem and its narrative setting. Bede suggests it when he mentions that in addition to Caedmon's paraphrase of Scripture and doctrine he also composed several songs "by which he sought to turn his hearers from delight in wickedness and to inspire them to love and do good." One thinks along this same line of Dante's letter to Can Grande della Scala in which he says that the aim of his great poem, in part and whole alike, is "to remove those living in this life from a state of misery and to bring them to a state of bliss." This is the same impetus that moves within the *Canterbury Tales*, the *Faerie Queene*, *Paradise Lost*, *Pilgrim's Progress:* the intention (through bawdry as well as beauty) to turn the reader from a delight in wickedness and inspire instead a desire to love and do good. Needless to say, the conversion of the reader is not all these works set out to do, nor can their artistry be reduced to a program in religious or moral instruction. But in the end their artistry is both instructive and heuristic; that is, it intends not only to recall the reader to truths forgotten, but also lead us to discover ourselves in God. Therefore the story of a man lost in a dark wood or of a gentle knight pricking on the plain are narratives which have in view what St. Paul speaks of in Romans as "the renewing of your minds." In this way the work moves in two directions at once, backward to the received teachings of Scripture and tradition and forward to the reader — a double movement of recollection and discovery.

For a text to function in these ways, however, certain conditions must be met. There needs to be a consensus between author and reader based on the shared possession of the biblical subtext, an agreement as to the verities which are to be recalled and about the nature of true self-discovery. In Bede's account of Caedmon, for instance, he presupposes a genuine continuity between the events of Scripture and the ongoing activity of God, so that the bashful singer can be represented as the fulfillment of scriptural typology, a present-day example of the Holy Spirit's divine influence. Bede also assumes that dreams are not simply occasions when one talks and listens to oneself, but times when one may genuinely receive the mysterious will of God, as did the patriarchs and apostles.

Presuppositions such as these, however, are ones which no contemporary writer can make, at least if he or she is looking for a major audience. Each of the authors to be dealt with in this book will variously understand the rupture between Bede's world and our own, either as a historical fact of changed human consciousness, as does Murdoch, or as a historical tragedy and a rupture with reality itself. Certainly the pathos of the break is most acutely expressed by O'Connor throughout her non-fictional prose. In *Mystery and Manners* she writes,

> For the last few centuries we have lived in a world which has been increasingly convinced that the reaches of reality are very close to the surface, that there is no ultimate divine source, that the things of the world do not pour forth from God. . . . For nearly two centuries the popular spirit of each succeeding generation had tended more and more to the view that the mysteries of life will eventually fall before modern man. . . . In twentieth century fiction it increasingly happens that a meaningless, absurd world impinges upon the sacred consciousness of author and character; author and character seldom now go out to explore and penetrate a world in which the sacred is reflected.
>
> (M 157-8)

In the following chapters we will see how O'Connor, Percy, and Murdoch challenge the prevailing notions of existence as shallow and impoverished, and in so doing go out to explore and penetrate the action of grace in their own varied terms. But for the moment I want to linger with the problem which confronts them: the struggle to suggest the resonance and depth of human life — what each refers to as "mystery" — when there is no authoritative story commonly held, no language for the realities that transcend our current theories. Both O'Connor and Percy see this as a profound crisis in the modern sensibility, this possibility (to quote Percy) "that man is presently undergoing a tempestuous restructuring of his consciousness which does not allow him to take account of the Good News . . . or God, the devil, and the angels if they were standing before him" (MB 113). Even from her own quite different perspective outside the Christian faith, Murdoch agrees with this diagnosis and likewise identifies the void at the center of our culture with the loss of religion as a consolation and guide: "A religious and moral vocabulary is the possession now of a very few; and most people lack the word with which to say just what is felt to be wrong is wrong."[2] One recalls O'Connor's more bitter observation about the generation of wingless chickens from which the moral sense has been bred out.

The problem, then, is twofold. First, how can you speak about the experience of grace without assuming a knowledge (let alone an acceptance) of any religious tradition, and, secondly, how can you speak engagingly about such an experience so as to open the reader to the sense of mystery and transcendence which the spirit of the present age has seemingly inoculated us against? Implicit in the latter half of this question, moreover, is the writer's desire not only to open the reader, but to move him or her in a particular direction. The writer desires so to alter consciousness that the Good News (or in Murdoch's case, the Good) can once again be taken into account and "what is felt to be wrong" spoken of as such. Clearly the danger here is that fiction will become the sugar coating on the pill, a way of getting a message across and down, rather than the creation of a world in which the experience of characters is as dense and ambiguous as our own — a believable world which offers the reader a chance for discovery rather than a lesson to be learned.

As we shall see in greater detail further on, there are different ways in which all three of these writers succumb to the temptation of didacticism. In O'Connor, it is often the tendency of the narrator to be too explicitly omniscient about the religious meaning of events, and in Percy and Murdoch it is the all too obvious presence of characters who serve to voice the author's ideas. In all three there is a contrivance of plot that sometimes bullies the reader into what can seem like a predestined corner. We can view these characteristics of their work as failures of skill or, on the other hand, as difficulties to be expected when communicating an alien vision of life. After all, the desire to shout, however it expresses itself, may inevitably result from the inability to be understood more naturally or unconsciously. In any event, what I am identifying here as occasional lapses should not discredit the ideal toward which O'Connor, Percy, and Murdoch all work, and which in their several ways they also more than occasionally attain. For they achieve a fiction that powerfully explores the mystery of human transformation, that surprises and disarms as much as it instructs, that awakens curiosity and longing within the reader which has perhaps been forgotten or never before been realized. It is a literature with designs upon the reader, but which at its best exerts its will indirectly and without coercion.

It may be useful in thinking about strategies of indirection to look briefly at a mode of literary discourse which, although very much within the biblical tradition, did not in the beginning share any kind of consensus with its audience. It is a mode of discourse that in fact often anticipates an unconvinced or even hostile reception. I am referring, of course, to the parables of Jesus, whose relevance to the fiction under discussion does not have to do with questions of influence or genre, but rather with the development of a language of grace. The parables serve, I think, as a paradigm within the ancient legacy of Scripture for the kind of contemporary literature to be explored in this study: secular fictions designed to involve their audience in sacred mysteries across a barrier of disagreement. For before they "became" the Bible, and therefore the hermeneutical property of a believing community, the stories which Jesus told were quite obviously not spoken to people who already shared his assumptions. A number of the parables presuppose sharp antagonism. Joachim Jeremias perhaps overstates the matter when he calls them "weapons of warfare," but the emphasis is, I think, correct.[3] The parables are meant not only to intimate a new and often disturbing notion of reality — the kingdom of God — but also to win over the persons who hear them against every resistance of nature and habit.

As important as the original polemic may have been in their formation, it is of greater interest in this context to consider how their particular warfare is accomplished. For the parables do their work indirectly, by inviting us to enter a narrative world where we must discover our own responses and make our own decisions. Thus, while a parable may very well be a "weapon of warfare" or a means of instruction, the response it calls for is a free one

— prepared for and primed, to be sure, but still one which is not coerced. Adolf Jülicher speaks of the parable's gentle renunciation of force as a kind of subtle seduction: on the one hand it is just a story, offered objectively as an event; on the other, it is a trap.[4] And yet the reader or listener who becomes enmeshed in the story's net, entangled, as it were, in its narrative law, is not held captive to an interpretation. The reader is compelled, rather, to encounter him- or herself.

The most dramatic instance of this entrapment in Scripture is Nathan's parable of the ewe lamb in 2 Samuel, where David, upon hearing the story of a rich man's appropriation of a poor man's meagre property, is lured into making a judgment on the story's villain which then redounds upon himself: "Nathan said to David, 'You are that man.' " But it is precisely the absence of a Nathan, an interpreter, that characterizes the parable itself. For while filled with moments of decision and judgment, there is no one within the narrative itself to bring the story home; there is only the person who listens or reads. "He that has eyes to see, let him see; and ears to hear, let him hear."

When we turn to the fiction of O'Connor, Percy, and Murdoch we will see the extent to which they realize the strategy of the parable-teller in their own attempts to "entrap" the reader into self-awareness. But here we should also note for future reference and comparison the way the parables present the action of grace to an audience whose faith cannot be assumed. While the ultimate referent of these stories may indeed be the divine-human relationship — the invisible mystery of grace working unseen within the visible universe — parables are, at least at first glance, singularly mundane in tone. They take place in the home, or at the job, or on the road in between; they deal with conflicts between family members, or between workers and their employer, or a ruler and his subjects; they portray a full range of recognizable human vices with occasional bright moments of generosity, mercy, and love; they delight in the unforeseen gift. Dan O. Via suggests that it is their lack of a specifically religious terminology that opens the parables to an entirely nonreligious interpretation accessible to anyone.

But if the strictly human or existentialist reading is so satisfying, what makes them parables of the kingdom of God? Why move from a literal to an anagogic level and interpret them as "religious" stories at all? In the first place, what appears to be nonreligious terminology taken from a strictly secular world is, in fact, rich in sacred association. The presentation of God as father, judge, and ruler, the suggestion of salvation through the setting of a feast or wedding, the identification of Israel as a vineyard — these are all traditional metaphors in Hebrew Scripture which inevitably contextualize the stories which incorporate them and add a resonance to their narrative. While this ancestry does not force a religious interpretation of the story, it provides the possibility (and perhaps even the likelihood) of just such a reading. Jesus could not presuppose in His listeners a belief in His authority, but He could count on a Jewish audience to hear the parables against the background of their own tradition.

In addition to the hermeneutical clues offered by metaphors that carry with them a sacred history, there is another verbal attribute of the parables which we may call their language of ultimacy. This is a sudden heightening of the story's normal level of discourse, which does not depend for its effectiveness on any previous knowledge of tradition. It is usually found at the end of a story, when the action is completed and its particularities are suddenly seen against a depth of mysterious implication. It occurs in the parable of the talents, for instance, after the master strips the "wicked and slothful servant" of his single uninvested coin: "For to everyone who has more will be given, and he will have abundance; but from him who has not, even what he has will be taken away" (Matt. 25.29). This statement has the authoritative ring of a proverb, an accepted bit of wisdom which pronounces upon the narrative without explanation or room for defense. One might say that it confuses the literal story by taking us away from the manageable specifics of master and servant, instead placing us before a law of awesome generality. Left with it, we begin to wonder if we understood what the story was really about, because clearly it makes far more of the servant's failure to invest the talent than the circumstances would realistically warrant — as if the issue had very little to do with money at all. Rather, the closing oppositions between abundance and poverty, gain and loss, seem to elevate the story beyond itself to some level of reality in which ultimate stakes are being played for and everything matters absolutely.

If we turn from the language of the parables to their dramatic structure, there is yet another way in which what O'Connor refers to as the "added dimension" of a story is suggested. What I am speaking of is the culmination of the parable in judgment, a decisive "end time" when the elements of the story are quickly brought together for some kind of resolution. In some instances the eschatology of the parable leads to a condemnation — the five foolish virgins (Matt. 25.1-13), the unforgiving servant (Lk. 18.23-35), the cautious man with one talent (Matt. 25.14-30) — when judgment suddenly brings the status quo into account, revealing human conduct for what it is in the eye of the judge, with no court of appeal to challenge his assessment.

Sometimes the narrative eschatology of the parable will be placed in a religious context by a concluding saying (often added by the evangelist) that links the story to a moment or event that stands outside it, as at the end of the parable of the talents: "And cast the worthless servant into outer darkness; there shall men weep and gnash their teeth" (Matt. 25.30). Via describes this joining together of parable and nonparabolic saying as an interpretive tug of war: the parable implies that the unrecoverable loss of existence happens in human history, while the saying pulls the parable out of the earthly continuum and into the mystery of God.[5] Looked at another way one could say that the parable dramatizes in earthly terms the inevitability of reckoning, while the saying reveals the moment of truth in its eternal consequences. Either way, however, we see the evangelist's desire to specify a religious meaning, to "locate" the narrative and interpret its eschatological crisis for the reader. Without the saying, the parable gives us nothing more nor less than a world in which people must come to terms with what they have or have not done. It is a world in which the end of the story brings with it a judgment on everything that has gone on before, indelibly marking whatever future one can imagine its characters to be entering.

In addition to these "tragic" parables, where trial and condemnation predominate, there are others in which the eschatological crisis of the narrative precipitates not a curse, but a blessing, where predictably bad events make an abrupt and unpredictable turn for the better. In stories of this kind what interrupts the normal course of affairs, and thereby implies "something more," is the sudden impact of the extraordinary and marvellous, with its overflowing sense of extravagance. Here the unforeseen turn of events is not ushered in by a bolt of retributive lightning, but rather by something like a stroke of good fortune from out of the blue. What also characterizes this windfall is that it is usually quite undeserved; indeed, the parables often heighten the sheer gratuity of the gift by portraying the unfairness of the bestowal upon ne'er-do-well sons and newcomers to the vineyard. Where one would legitimately expect justice and therefore condemnation, one encounters instead a mercy and generosity that disturb our notions of what is supposed to be. And it is in that shock to our sensibilities that the comic parables, like the tragic, challenge all our preconceptions of reality that do not admit this wonderful suspension of "realism."

Nonetheless we have to ask whether the suspension of realism will necessarily indicate the presence of God or the action of grace for anyone who is not already seeking it, who is not already looking in the direction to which the parable is pointing. If we are not told that the discovery of a treasure buried in a field has something to do with the kingdom of heaven, why would we understand it to be so? The teller of the story always runs the risk of not being understood in full or even at all, no matter how many clues are left along the way. This risk seems, in fact, to be in the nature of the parable form itself. For it places a premium on the freedom of the reader to come to an interpretive decision of his or her own, that is, to discover the transforming depth of the story — or not.

It is with this liability in mind that we turn to the fiction of O'Connor, Percy, and Murdoch. In these last pages I have stressed the peculiar relationship which the teller of the parable must establish with the audience, in order to highlight the situation of these contemporary writers. The similarity lies in their desire to overcome opposition and resistance, to communicate an alien vision by indirect means, all to the end of bringing the reader to a new state of consciousness and self-awareness. But there are other resemblances as well. O'Connor's stories, with their remarkable concision and quality of paradox, most obviously recall not only parabolic form, but the stark intensity of atmosphere as well. All three writers share a penchant for the shattering of the status quo as a prelude to transformation, such as we find in many of the parables, both tragic and comic. They also hold in common a choice of language which more or less openly inflects the transcendent into an otherwise secular narrative, and a predilection for extraordinary turns of plot, as well as for startling "end time" crises that suddenly bring down a confusion of judgment and blessing. These writers will differ from one another in their use of such parabolic techniques, but each will work to disorient the reader through miracles and mysteries of storytelling precisely in order to bring about some basic reorientation of vision. The degree to which this handling of the reader becomes a manipulation indicates, perhaps, the degree to which these writers fail not simply to sustain their strategy of indirection, but to heal the breach in communication that stretches between writer and audience. In any event, their search to discover a new language of grace deserves the respect paid to those who undertake the most difficult of tasks, for what they seek to do is nothing less than to bridge the great gulf fixed between ourselves and the realities we can no longer speak about.

2 Flannery O'Connor

Despite her sarcastic rejection of any notion of the writer as one who suffers in lonely isolation from the uncomprehending crowd, it is impossible to read Flannery O'Connor's nonfictional prose without being struck by the fact that almost every reference to the reader assumes an inability to understand her work. To begin with, there is in *The Habit of Being* her exasperated characterization of the average Catholic as a "Militant Moron" (L 179) looking for "positive" fiction that will provide the Instant Answer. One essay in *Mystery and Manners* mentions the Catholic reader's penchant for writers who will rearrange reality according to stock theological principles, getting themselves "as little dirty in the process as possible" (M 163). But because the reader for whom O'Connor wrote was not Catholic but pagan, both her irritation and her concern were primarily reserved for those whom the Scholastics would have called the invincibly ignorant: the majority of contemporary readers of fiction who, in O'Connor's opinion, were not adequately equipped to believe anything at all. Nor is this characterization of the reader limited to the widows, convicts, and sanitarium inmates whose correspondence (and criticism) she despaired of. It also typified the contemporary literary establishment, perhaps personified for her by Van Wyck Brooks, who after hearing her read "A Good Man Is Hard To Find," commented that it was a shame someone with so much talent should look upon life as a horror story.[1]

How O'Connor looked upon life is in one sense very clear, as we know from her frequent and explicit references to her faith. Indeed, she made the issue of her own beliefs an unavoidable consideration, even though in doing so she opened herself to religious overinterpretation: "No one thinks you can lift the pen without trying to show someone redeemed" (L 434). Her Catholicism was an orthodoxy that reflects the period just before the Second Vatican Council, but it is of a piece with that tradition of intellect and imagination which we saw in Bede's account of Caedmon. Expressed in the doctrines of the Fall, Redemption, and Judgment, O'Connor's Catholicism is centered in the Incarnation of Christ. It affirms the freedom of all persons to accept or reject God's grace, with each one's choice confirmed by God at death for eternity.[2]

While this summary might just as well describe the theological assumptions of a Christian classic such as the *Divine Comedy*, O'Connor's theologial conservatism only highlights the radically different climate in which the contemporary Christian writer works — and which she in particular worked against. For what separates her situation from Dante's is not only that her basic beliefs were not shared; they were, she thought, not even intelligible to the average reader. Thus she expected that her novel *The Violent Bear It Away* would get "trounced" by reviewers unable to understand its most basic referents: "Besides the fact that nobody knows about the devil now, I have to reckon on the fact that baptism is just another idiocy to the gentle reader. . ." (L 373). Unlike the writer in an age of faith, she needed not only to create a believable fictive world, but to develop as well the sense of a Creator working behind, within, and beyond it. Or, as she expresses her mandate to "A" in terms even more difficult to satisfy, "the writer has to succeed in making the divinity of Christ seem consistent with the structure of all reality" (L 290).

For Dante this could be done directly, as at the end of *Paradiso* when the pilgrim sees at the center of a trinity of concentric circles *la nostra effige,* our incarnate image — the divinity of Christ consistent with the structure of reality. This O'Connor could not show the reader, any more than she could portray a spiritual odyssey as a journey through the afterlife. Instead, she had to discover her vocation as a Catholic writer who (as she first presented herself to "A") was "peculiarly possessed by the modern consciousness, that thing Jung describes as unhistorical, solitary and guilty. To possess this *within* the Church is to bear a burden, the necessary burden for the conscious Catholic. It is to feel the contemporary situation at the ultimate level" (L 90).

There is no evidence in anything O'Connor wrote which would lead us to assume that the contemporary burden to which she alludes here is religious doubt. Rather it is, I think, the task of portraying reality as it is present to the modern consciousness that possesses all of us — cut off from history, locked into isolation and guilt, with no fixed reference point, and no real sense of spiritual need. And it is by starting there, where she thought us collectively to be, that she would try to show the divine image at the heart of things, not face to face, but reflected in our broken condition. To feel the contemporary situation at the ultimate level is to be in the world but not of it; it is to suffer the blindness of the reader in order to generate the longing for light.

O'Connor's strategy for approaching her audience begins with the establishing of a recognizably real world, a "nature" which we can acknowledge to be our own. This is not simply because we are physical beings, intelligible to one another only through our senses, nor is it only because O'Connor saw the aim of the novelist (in a phrase borrowed from Joseph Conrad) as rendering "the highest possible justice to the physical universe" (M 80). It is because O'Connor knew that if her fiction was to convey the action of the supernatural to readers predisposed to admit no such thing, it would have to locate the mystery of grace in the solid flesh of our experience, within the social conventions or "manners" that exemplify and evoke an everyday life. To accomplish this she would look at farmyard or small town with the eye of a satirist who misses no detail or nuance or trick, and a satirist also gifted with a fine ear for the conventional phrase, the odd word, the rhythm and color of ordinary speech.

But most of all O'Connor would establish the reality of her fictive world through humor, through the laughter of recognition that creates a bond of familiarity between ourselves and her characters that somehow turns our amusement over them into a kinship with them — as if we all came from the same place. This ability not only to make us see, but to make us laugh at what we see, accounts to a great degree for the verisimilitude of her fiction. And nowhere is it more powerfully apparent than in the similes that at once focus, satirize, and endear the characters they describe to us, as in this portrayal of Julian and his mother from "Everything That Rises Must Converge":

> The lighted bus appeared on the top of the next hill and as it approached, they moved out into the street to meet it. He put his hand under her elbow and hoisted her up on the creaking step. She entered with a little smile, as if she were going into a drawing room where everyone had been waiting for her.
>
> (CS 410)

We know that bus, that hand under the plump elbow, the parlor pretentions of this undefeated if overweight "belle" making an event out of an otherwise bare moment. O'Connor's humor seduces the reader into her world. It encourages us to let our guard down, to feel comfortable and relaxed and ready for what the narrative will bring.

If the way to introduce the reader to the supernatural is first through the literal level of natural events, the comic "letter" of the text is at the same time a means to another end. For while O'Connor's intention may well have been to render the highest possible justice to the physical universe, she does so by portraying the material world as a gateway to the spiritual realm that at once inhabits and transcends it. This is not to say that she meant the physical to be disposed of, like the chaff around the wheat, but only that it be stared at in order to see within it signs of an invisible struggle with or against grace — a struggle that is the central event of her fiction. Because of the priority of the spiritual as the force that animates the body, the cause that has its effects, she intends the literal level of her work to bespeak the allegorical, manners to reveal mystery, nature to open to grace, and the countryside in which we live our mundane lives to dissolve into the True Country which is absolute and eternal.

These paired distinctions reflect O'Connor's traditional Christian sensibility; they would make perfect sense to Dante or Aquinas. And yet such distinctions can easily be construed as oppositions, as when Joyce Carol Oates speaks of O'Connor's "essentially Manichean dualism of the Secular and the Sacred," where "the natural ordinary world is either sacramental (and ceremonial) or profane (and vulgar)."[3] What Oates fails to grasp is the unity in which the apparent dualities of nature and grace actually cohere. For O'Connor, the ordinary vulgar world *is* sacramental: it is the place where God is present, in circus sideshows and tattoo parlors and pigpens. This world is profane only when it is viewed as independent of its divine source, and therefore cut off from its true identity as a creation — just as a sign becomes free-floating and then meaningless when it loses its attachment to its referent. For O'Connor secularity is a point of view, and one as old as the Fall itself.

What is distinctive about the modern era is that the conflict between nature and grace has been resolved by the elimination of the notion of grace altogether. Thus, if O'Connor sets out to renew the battle by making what Oates refers to as brutal distinctions between the City of God and the City of Man, it is not only to reintroduce the sacred into our consciousness, but to reintegrate it with our assumptions about the natural and ordinary. The warfare she wages is not, in fact, spirit against flesh, but, rather, spirit *in* flesh. Her goal is not only to make it impossible to deny the sacred as present in the midst of the secular; it is to make it impossible to rest easy with any notion of secularity at all.

O'Connor considered her fiction realistic and herself a "realist of distances" (M 44, 179). What this difficult phrase points to, I think, is a vision of reality which detects the invisible world fomenting within the visible, a way of seeing "near things with their extensions of meaning and thus of seeing far things close up" (M 44): in other words, it is no conventional notion of realism at all. One could as easily speak of her work as comedy of manners, though with a similar and drastic reorientation of expectations. For however ably O'Connor evokes a believable world through close observation and humor, she does not flesh out her characters against a detailed background of psychology and society, such as we expect to find in realistic fiction. Considerations like these are "mere problems" to her, and she passes them by with no compunction. The background she ushers us into is not primarily the private history of her characters, nor the social setting in which they live, nor anything else by which we might normally explain a person; rather, it is the mystery of existence which each of us stumbles upon at birth — the mystery which she believed to be our relationship with God. O'Connor brings her characters to the point where they can avoid that relationship no longer, though often they do not understand its meaning. They walk out on thin ice, suddenly to fall into a depth they never knew was there. It is the "added dimension" of everyday life to which they are blind and oblivious, until the surface cracks, splits, and abandons them to a profundity of experience they cannot escape or explain away.

Such "distances" are presumably as unknown to O'Connor's hypothetical reader as they are to her characters up until their moment of truth. Thus the realism which at once scans the surface and plumbs the depths is almost exclusively the possession of the narrator herself, and a gift her fiction struggles continually to impart. How O'Connor carried on that struggle and her success in doing so can be seen when we turn to the twenty-odd short stories and two novels which comprise her literary oeuvre. Within that body of work, the place to begin is with her particular countryside, the South. While it is true for every writer that "somewhere is better than anywhere" (M 200), the South offered O'Connor not only a single place — and the place she knew best — but a region peculiarly saturated with the Christian religion: hardly Christ-centered, she admits, but certainly Christ-haunted.[4] The pieces collected in *Mystery and Manners* explore this haunting in various ways. Because it retains the Bible as a cultural subtext, the South is able to read its own small history, complete with the Fall and with an "inburnt knowledge of human limitations" (M 59), within a universal context. With the sacred story continuing to be common cultural property, however attenuated or bizarre its appropriations, the ordinary person is still, at least potentially, able to see personal action under the aspect of eternity. Belief remains believable, and for this reason the region offers the Christian writer a unique opportunity: "Religious enthusiasm is accepted as one of the South's more grotesque features, and it is possible to build upon that acceptance, however little real understanding such acceptance may carry with it" (M 204).

What the South gave O'Connor is a countryside that has not lost touch with the True Country, where the surface of the landscape is marked by signs of the depths, whether they be the roadside reminders of salvation or the gospel music carrying its radio message even into the doctor's waiting room. Within this landscape there are religious enthusiasts driven to extremes by their strange faith: characters like Hazel Motes, or Tarwater, or Mrs. Greenleaf shrieking "Jesus, stab me in the heart!" as she flails about in the dirt. But far more pervasive is the presence of Christianity as something in the back of the mind, or, thoughtlessly, on the tip of the tongue, a part of the cultural atmosphere no more consciously attended to than the air her characters breathe — until, breathless, they are forced by circumstances to pay attention, and the dead cliché in their chatter becomes a living, if dreadful, truth.

O'Connor's fictive world is also populated by figures who pride themselves on having put behind ignorance and superstition entirely, a New South of school teachers and social workers, of sturdy middle-class women like Mrs. McIntyre in "The Displaced Person," about whom, we are told, "Christ in the conversation embarrassed her the way sex had her mother" (CS 226). This breed is often a younger generation scowling at the instinctive religion of their parents or social inferiors, like Tanner's New York City daughter in "The Last Judgement" who pleads with her father, "If you would let me pull your chair around to look at the TV, you would quit thinking about morbid stuff, death and hell and judgement. My Lord." (CS 541)

Presumably the mind of this modern South is also what O'Connor imagined her typical reader to resemble, the generation of wingless chickens for whom God is dead. And it is precisely these characters, with whom her audience might be expected to identify, whom O'Connor brings into calamity so dire that the confident secularity of their lives is shattered by experiences with which they have no way of coping. It is then, stripped bare and defenseless, that they are left with nothing but the old-time religion they had thought dead, or at least buried in the ignorance of the countryside, nailed to pine trees along the highway: "DOES SATAN HAVE YOU IN HIS POWER? REPENT OR BURN IN HELL. JESUS SAVES" (CS 450-1). Thus Sheppard, having told Rufus Johnson in "The Lame Shall Enter First" that such talk was complete rubbish — "We're living in the space age!" — comes by the end of the story to a very different perception: "He saw the clear-eyed Devil, the sounder of hearts, leering at him from the eyes of Johnson. His image of himself shrivelled until everything was black before him. He sat there paralyzed, aghast" (CS 481).

Whether or not the reader also comes to such a vision is, of course, another question. But within the world of the story, Sheppard's discovery of evil — not only in Rufus Johnson, but in himself — suggests that the religious understanding of life he had relegated to the dark ages (and back roads) of the Old South may be, in fact, a viable description of reality. O'Connor's choice of this region as her fictional setting enables her to keep religion on the surface of her work, available to her characters as a way to understand the depths into which they fall. It is often as if the background music they had either ignored or tried very hard not to listen to suddenly became the only sound to hear.

But if the South by virtue of its religious consciousness provided O'Connor with a natural world haunted by grace, the fact remains that she does not portray her characters' experience of the transcendent within that world as anything "natural" at all. Rather, her stories routinely destroy the sense of the ordinary they have sought to create. Characters typically hurtle toward some extraordinary crisis in which the breakthrough of insight, if it occurs at all, entails the utter breakdown of the normal and everyday — even, on occasion, the end of such existence entirely. In a number of her works, though not in all, O'Connor deliberately cultivates the bizarre and grotesque. She would shock rather than surprise; she chooses the situation *in extremis,* the self-mutilation, the goring by a bull, the child's head smashed against a rock.

There are a number of ways in which O'Connor accounts for this preference and its place in her work. On the one hand, she says that the grotesque incarnates the illness of the human condition, the extent to which we have fallen from the image of God in which we were created. In other words, it shows us that there is something radically *wrong.* On the other hand, she maintains that the grotesque expresses the tension and discrepancies that arise when grace is at work in a nature that either resists it or is struggling to comply: it reveals the creation in travail, awaiting its redemption. She also states, quite apart from this usage *in bono* and *in malo,* that the grotesque is simply the nature of her particular talent, the sheer penchant of her imagination. This is, perhaps, the truest account.

What interests us most here, however, is the fact that O'Connor views the grotesque as a primary way to reach the unbelieving reader:

> When you can assume your audience holds the same beliefs you do, you can relax a little and use more normal means of talking to it; when you have to assume that it does not, then you have to make your

> vision apparent by shock — to the hard of hearing you shout, and for the almost-blind you draw large and startling figures. (M 34)

Elsewhere she speaks of the need to generate enough awe and mystery around an event in order to demonstrate that it is ultimately significant. Distortion and exaggeration, then, become her means of revelation, because above all she has to "make the reader feel, in his bones if nowhere else, that something is going on here that counts" (M 162).

This last reference pertains directly to Tarwater's baptismal drowning of the idiot child Bishop: the end toward which she bends the language, structure, and action of her novel *The Violent Bear It Away.* But certainly her inclination toward "shouting," as well as her preference for the exaggerated and distorted, consistently characterize the moments in her fiction when distances collapse and mystery engulfs manners. Sometimes this moment is an actual epiphany, such as that occasioned by the chipped piece of lawn statuary in "The Artificial Nigger" or by the sideshow hermaphrodite in "A Temple of the Holy Ghost." Often, however, the revelation is nothing more (though clearly nothing less) than an awareness of personal emptiness and vanity, as when Julian taunts his mother into a heart attack and finds himself adrift in a "tide of darkness," or when Hulga in "Good Country People" loses her artificial leg to a lascivious Bible salesman — and with it, her proud identity.

Brief synopses such as these remind us of the weird ends to which O'Connor drives her stories. We can begin to understand her strange penchant for violence as a way of suggesting the intense struggle between the divine will and characters like Julian and Hulga, who are little disposed to cooperate with it. Their egos have elaborate defenses and must, therefore, be forcibly broken into. For this reason the kingdom will often come with weeping and gnashing of teeth, and the intervention of grace appear like a murderous assault, the end of life rather than a beginning. "In my stories," she writes, "I have found that violence is strangely capable of returning my characters to reality and preparing them to accept their moment of grace. Their heads are so hard that almost nothing else will do the work."[5]

If this divine breaking and entering is what O'Connor intended her characters' bizarre experiences to signify, it is also apparent that the almost blind and the hard of hearing did not always take it so. Like some of the victims in O'Connor's stories, they were not quite certain what had hit them. Her reactions to what she considered to be misreading of her work often took the form of pique "at an audience who doesn't know what grace is and don't recognize it when they see it" (L 275). What O'Connor meant to be the story of a conversion, *they* mistook for madness and degeneracy — or had no use for at all. And yet, of course, the danger she ran in drawing large and startling figures was precisely the loss of that credibility which she also knew to be her essential bond with the non-believing reader. Shouting, it turns out, may very well be the least likely way to be heard.

There are indications in her correspondence that she realized this to be true. For instance, she agreed with one critic of the collection *A Good Man Is Hard To Find* that it is difficult to sustain interest in characters who relate directly to God unless they are shown to be very human — characters and not caricatures — and vowed that her second novel, *The Violent Bear It Away*, would be "more human, less farcical" (L 111). She subsequently confided that while her presentations of grace needed to compete in violence and drama with the kind of evil she was able to make concrete, she also wanted to explore new possibilities of understatement: "I keep seeing Elias in the cave, waiting to hear the voice of the Lord in the thunder and lightning and wind, and only hearing it finally in the gentle breeze, and I feel I'll have to be able to do that sooner or later, or anyway keep trying. . ." (L 373).

If the grotesque furnished O'Connor with a mixed blessing — a startling rhetorical strategy, but one which often worked at cross purposes with itself — she relied more successfully on her narratorial voice to suggest the ultimate meaning of her stories. Although she confides to "A" that "point of view runs me nuts!", the viewpoint which she used throughout her work to great advantage was the omniscient narrator who speaks a story into being with no inflection of personal consciousness whatsoever. Its effect is to make the stories appear to be descriptions of reality, the way things are, despite the stylization and strangeness of the fiction itself.

The crucial importance of the narrator in suggesting the "added dimension" can best be seen if we extract her dialogue from its narrative context and thereby silence the author's interpretive voice. An example of this elimination is afforded by John Huston's 1979 film version of *Wise Blood.* The screenplay is meticulously faithful to the dialogue of the book, but because we are given *only* the dialogue we find ourselves left with what the characters can understand and express on their own. Without the narrator we remain outside the significance of the action — engaged, to be sure, but aware only of what the characters themselves can convey to us. And since O'Connor's fiction is filled with figures who act largely on impulse, with little or no conscious perspective on their actions, our own vision is drastically reduced to theirs. The camera in this case cannot be said actually to lie, but we are nonetheless left with half a book and no way to read it aright.

This is nowhere more apparent than at the end of the film, when Mrs. Flood bends over the burned-out eyes of Hazel Motes' corpse, unaware that he is dead. "I knew you'd come back," she said. "And I've been waiting for you. And you needn't to pay any more rent but have it free here any way you like, upstairs or down. Just however you want it and with me to wait on you, or if you want to go somewhere, we'll both go."

By this point, our view of Mrs. Flood has already changed from that of a cartoon landlady, mercenary and suspicious, to a pathetic old woman offering herself as a "home" and a "place" in an otherwise desolate world. Motes gives her no more encouragement in death than in life, but her need is such that she will settle for a blank stare and no rent, anything rather than nothing. Her words spoken to the dead man are at once poignant and absurd, Southern Gothic with touches of hometown existentialism (" 'There's nothing, Mr. Motes,' she said").

Mrs. Flood's words leave us with a very dark comedy indeed — a woman making plans with a corpse. Quite unlike the film, however, the novel does not end with a close-up of an old woman staring into the empty eye sockets of her would-be lover; rather, the narrator enables us to see what the camera cannot record, that this apparent dead end is, in fact, a place to begin.

> She had never observed his face more composed and she grabbed his hand and held it to her heart. It was resistless and dry. The outline of the skull was plain under his skin and the deep burned eye sockets seemed to lead into the dark tunnel where he had disappeared.

> She leaned closer and closer to his face, looking deep into them, trying to see how she had been cheated or what had cheated her, but she couldn't see anything. She shut her eyes and saw the pinpoint of light but so far away that she could not hold it steady in her mind. She felt as if she were blocked at the entrance of something. She sat staring with her eyes shut, into his eyes, and felt as if she had finally gotten to the beginning of something she couldn't begin, and she saw him moving farther and farther away, farther and farther into the darkness until he was the pinpoint of light.
>
> (WB 231-2)

The novel ends with the narrator's enlargement of Mrs. Flood's situation far beyond her powers of consciousness and expression, deeper and further into her experience than she herself is able to go. We see from a vantage above the old woman's sight, from a higher point of view, even as O'Connor's narratorial prose elevates from the flatness of speech to language that is far richer in metaphor and suggestiveness. The lady wants a companion, but we are led to understand that what she truly seeks is more profound than company. For as the life of Hazel Motes seems to disappear down a dark tunnel before which she stalls, "at the beginning of something she couldn't begin," he becomes the pinpoint of light at the tunnel's end, at once describing the great distance between them and providing her with a beacon, something to move toward.

It is there, on the brink of a journey that seems it is going nowhere but to death, that we remember what the narrator has told us before, when Mrs. Flood first pondered Hazel's blindness and the funny way he looked, always straining forward.

> She imagined it was like you were walking in a tunnel

> and all you could see was a pinpoint of light. She had to imagine the pinpoint of light; she couldn't think of it at all without that. She saw it as some kind of star, like the star on Christmas cards. She saw him going backwards to Bethlehem and she had to laugh.
>
> (WB 218-19)

More akin to Yeats' rough beast slouching toward Bethlehem than any biblical wise man, Hazel Motes nonetheless provides Mrs. Flood with her initiation into mystery. He takes her from darkness to light, from death to the possibility of birth. This is something that *we* know, but that she does not. And to follow this interpretation we must follow the lead of the narrator, for it is she who sees deeper and further into Hazel's Church Without Christ and Mrs. Flood's "not believing in Jesus," and discovers both characters moving backwards to Bethlehem. Using O'Connor's own vocabulary, we might say that it is the narrator who calls attention to the invisible action of grace within the visible narrative.

As we see above with the image of the star, O'Connor will often use biblical allusion to place the events of her story into an explicitly religious context, thereby inviting readers to see more there than they otherwise might. In "Parker's Back," for instance, OE's exploded tractor affords a vision of a "tree of fire and his empty shoe burning beneath it" — a not very veiled reference to the theophany of Exodus 3, where Moses stands barefoot to receive Yahweh's call before the burning bush. More explicit still is the comparison of the pool hall from which OE is ejected to "the ship from which Jonah had been cast into the sea."

In both of the above instances O'Connor is relating the more or less comic experience of a backwoods tattoo fetishist to that same biblical typology exploited by Bede in his account of Caedmon: the reluctant prophet who is called not only against his wishes, but in this case totally beyond his comprehension. The tawdriness of the story's setting, and the low humor of OE and his wife Sarah Ruth, seem to pull against this traditional thematic substructure. And yet the tension between the ridiculous and the sublime is itself part of the biblical tradition, with its preference for the tent and stable, the family squabbles and criminal's death, as the chosen meeting place of the human and divine. It comes as no surprise, therefore, to learn that O'Connor delighted in one critic's view that the best of her work "sounded like the Old Testament would if it were being written today" (L 111). For in O'Connor's fiction, as in the Scriptures, we find ourselves in a narrative world where the lowest experience bears the most exalted burden and our view of human action is projected against the obscure background of God's will.

O'Connor's use of biblical allusion or overtly religious language will often intensify toward the end of a work, at the point where she goes for "altitude" or a "larger view" for a way to raise the narrative above its particular human confines and reveal it *sub specie aeternitatis.* At times it will appear as an enlargement of the protagonist's own consciousness, as when the child in "A Temple of the Holy Ghost" drives away from Benediction and sees the evening sun "like an elevated Host drenched in blood," or when Asbury in "The Enduring Chill" recognizes the Holy Spirit, fierce and implacable, descending upon him from the bird-like stain above his sickbed. Certainly the most splendid example is Ruby Turpin's vision at the conclusion of "Revelation," when the earthly hierarchies that we have seen dominate her approach to life throughout the story are marvellously reversed, although with no loss of glory for the first who shall be last.

But if in the closing pages of "Revelation" O'Connor is able to show us how the last shall be first and the first last, the narrator's eleventh-hour use of biblical language or allusion is not always successful. Rather than seeming an inevitable expression of the story, her signalling of the added dimension can appear added on, an imposition of grace upon nature that makes the introduction of the religious seem overstated or arbitrary — another way to shout at the hard of hearing, to make sure the reader gets where the story means to go. Far from any simple failure of art, O'Connor's occasional overstatement of the religious grows out of her profound uneasiness with her readers. How could they be expected to know unless they were told? And how, with characters so caught up in the bewildering mystery of their own experience, how could they be told except by the narrator?

An example of this problem is provided by the ending of O'Connor's otherwise flawless story "The Artifical Nigger," where Mr. Head and his grandson Nelson, in a state of profound alienation from one another, suddenly come up short before a piece of lawn statuary as familiar to us as it is foreign to their country experience.

> The two of them stood there with their necks forward at almost the same angle and their shoulders curved in almost exactly the same way and their hands trembling identically in their pockets. Mr. Head looked like an ancient child and Nelson like a miniature old man. They stood gazing at the artificial Negro as if they were faced with some great mystery, some monument to another's victory that brought them together in their common defeat. They could feel it dissolving their differences like an action of mercy. Mr. Head had never known before what mercy felt like because he had been too good to deserve any, but he felt he knew now. He looked at Nelson and understood that he must say something to the child to show that he was still wise and in the look the boy returned

> he saw the need for that assurance. Nelson's eyes seemed to implore him to explain once and for all the mystery of existence.
>
> Mr. Head opened his lips to make a lofty statement and heard himself say, 'They ain't got enough real ones here. They got to have an artificial one.'
>
> After a second, the boy nodded with a strange shivering about his mouth, and said, 'Let's go home before we get ourselves lost again.'
>
> (CS 268-9)

At the outset of this extraordinary encounter O'Connor has her two characters confront themselves not as they would appear, but as they are: broken, ridiculous, as wildly miserable as the dilapidated racist cliché in front of them. But somehow in the presence of the statue that likeness to one another, which has fuelled an ongoing rivalry between them throughout the story, becomes for the first time an opportunity for peace: the artificial Negro is a "monument to another's victory that brought them together in their common defeat." Whose victory is that? We are not told, but are given instead a figure without form or comeliness, despised and rejected of men — what may be a grotesque image of the Crucified One. At first glance this demeaning caricature of a black man is, like the cross, a symbol of human as well as historical defeat. And yet in the mystery of grace — the mystery into which the story draws us — that stumbling block and offense becomes as well a victory, uniting the two cantankerous Heads in their lostness. In that coming together it offers them forgiveness, as layers of enmity dissolve between them "like an action of mercy."

O'Connor does not tell the reader that the artificial Negro is an image of Christ; rather, the power of the association lies in its being inherent and therefore unexpressed.

We are not told what the statue means, we are only shown what it does. Meaning is inherent in narrative action, as well as in the resonance of such phrases as "some great mystery," "action of mercy," and "the mystery of existence." Christ's redemption is a *hidden* presence.

This is not where O'Connor ends the story, however. Instead she takes Mr. Head (as she wrote to a friend) "from the Garden of Eden to the Gates of Paradise" (L 78) — an attempt to "elevate" the story and reveal what might otherwise be hidden from the reader.

> Mr. Head stood very still and felt the action of mercy touch him again, but this time he knew there were no words in the world to name it. He understood that it grew out of agony, which is not denied to any man and which is given in strange ways to children. He understood it was all a man could carry into death to give his Maker and he suddenly burned with shame that he had so little to take with him. He stood appalled, judging himself with the thoroughness of God, while the action of mercy covered his pride like a flame and consumed it. He had never thought himself a great sinner before but he saw now his true depravity had been hidden from him lest it cause him despair. He realized he was forgiven for sins from the beginning of time, when he conceived in his heart the sin of Adam, until the present, when he denied poor Nelson. He saw that no sin was too monstrous for him to claim as his own, and since God loved in proportion as He forgave, he felt ready at that instant to enter Paradise.
>
> (CS 270)

This concluding theological postscript seems to me to violate O'Connor's own conviction that at the end of a story there must always be left over "that sense of Mystery which cannot be accounted for by any human formula" (M 153). After Mr. Head's recital of salvation history, however, there is simply not enough left over: too many words have named it. Not only has Mr. Head been credited with a depth of religious understanding heretofore unseen in the story, but the reader has been forced to see and understand with him — a double coercion. This is because O'Connor is afraid to allow the reader to make his or her own discovery, to read a parable of grace without an interpretation. In leaving us with Nelson's "Let's go home before we get ourselves lost again," she would have run the risk of not conveying the fullness of the revealed faith or of leaving the unbeliever entirely behind, at sea in the "mystery of existence." What we would have had, on the other hand, is the sense of an encounter with reality too real for humans to bear for very long, but an encounter which nonetheless changes those who were there. She would have left her reader with the dangerous freedom to make of the story what he or she would.[6]

O'Connor exemplifies the dilemma of a writer who wants to communicate a mystery clearly, to write Christian fiction for a non-Christian audience. Indeed, this quandary is one of the abiding preoccupations of her correspondence, as in the letter to "A" where she confides her disappointment with the ending of "The Displaced Person" and what she considered to be its failure — her inability to show as purgatorial Mrs. McIntyre's wordless suffering over her complicity in the death of Mr. Guizac. She felt she had lost her audience, who could not be counted on to believe in God in the first place, let alone in the reality of

Purgatory. "None of this was adequately shown and to make the story complete it would have to be. . . . Understatement was not enough. However, there is certainly no reason why the effects of redemption must be plain to us and I think they usually are not" (L 118). Pulled in two different directions, serving two masters, she felt herself accountable both to the limitations of her reader and to the illimitable reality of her subject matter. It is no wonder that she thought there could be no great religious fiction without the combination of believing artist and believing society, for only then could the writer be ambiguous without forfeiting the understanding of her audience.[7]

This forfeiture, the price she would pay for indirection, can perhaps best be illustrated by the climactic moment in "A Good Man Is Hard To Find," a story about a family's disastrous trip to Florida that O'Connor frequently used in public readings and which consequently generated a good deal of comment, both from her and from the many who did not read it her way. The moment in question occurs at the end of the story but has been anticipated since the opening paragraph, where the narrator tells us that the grandmother of the family does not want her son, daughter-in-law, and two grandchildren to vacation in Florida because that is where a notorious criminal, The Misfit, is reputedly on his way. The real reason has to do with the Grandmother's entirely personal desire to visit her "connections" in East Tennessee instead, but from the very beginning her use of the outlaw as a pretext forges a vague association between the two of them, a connection to be realized quite concretely at the first climax of the story when an automobile accident on a dirt road detour suddenly deposits the family on the doorstep of The Misfit's hideout. What may seem too outrageous a coincidence outside the story appears somehow fated within it. Both the idea for the detour and the cause of the accident are utlimately the Grandmother's doing. She also brings The Misfit into the conversation at a roadside luncheonette — provoking Red Sammy, the owner, to reflect, "A good man is hard to find. Everything is getting terrible" — and then identifies him at the scene of the accident, with fatal results for the entire family. It seems, in fact, as if these two characters were meant to meet, as if they *had* to — and indeed O'Connor is counting on this sense of inevitability to transfer the story's suspense from surface to interior, from questions about what will happen to real curiosity about why it is happening. The story all but forces us to look for something crucial to come of their meeting.

What eventually does take place at the end of the narrative occurs only after a lengthy exchange between the two, as the other members of the family are led off in pairs to be shot. The Grandmother cajoles and flatters The Misfit in an attempt to save her family, much as we have seen her manipulating that same family beforehand. She is a "lady" and plays the part, just as she has been careful to dress for it before setting out on the trip. She knows he wouldn't ever *shoot* a lady, that he is a "good man," from "nice people," with "not a bit of common blood." But he will have none of her genteel nonsense, and her attempts to use "goodness" to disarm him fall as flat as her use of religion for the same purpose.

> "Do you ever pray?" she asked.
>
> He shook his head. All she saw was the black hat wiggle between his shoulder blades. "Nome," he said.
>
> . . . .
>
> "If you would pray," the old lady said, "Jesus would help you."
>
> "That's right," The Misfit said.
>
> "Well then, why don't you pray?" she asked trembling with delight suddenly.

> "I don't want no hep," he said. "I'm doing all right by myself."
>
> . . . .
>
> She wanted to tell him that he must pray. She opened and closed her mouth several times before anything came out. Finally she found herself saying, "Jesus, Jesus," meaning Jesus will help you, but the way she was saying it sounded as if she might be cursing.
>
> "Yes'm," The Misfit said as if he agreed. "Jesus thrown everything off balance. . . . If He did what He said, then it's nothing for you to do but throw away everything and follow Him, and if He didn't, then it's nothing for you to do but to enjoy the few minutes you got left the best way you can — by killing somebody or burning down his house or doing some other meanness to him. No pleasure but meanness," he said and his voice had become almost a snarl.
>
> (CS 129-32)

There are two things to notice in this protracted exchange. The first is the fact that The Misfit is Christ-haunted (if not Christ-centered), and wholly possessed by a radical sense of the gospel as a sternly either/or proposition. A decision about Jesus determines everything else, and he has said no to Jesus while convinced that the only alternative is as vehement a yes. The Misfit has made his choice and consequently there is no pleasure but meanness. In contrast the Grandmother introduces religion into her bargaining almost as if it were a card up her sleeve, played when everything else has failed. She tells him that he could be honest if he tried — "Think how wonderful it would be to settle down and live a comfortable life" — and to that Kiwanis Club end she tells him to pray, although we sense that he knows more what prayer really entails than she does. The Misfit won't ask for help because he knows he will not take it.

In addition to the different ways in which they each talk about religion — he as a profound unbeliever, she as a superficial Christian — we also observe how the Grandmother gradually associates The Misfit with her son. The two are initially juxtaposed when Bailey Boy curses his mother for having publicly recognized the criminal, and The Misfit attempts to comfort her: " 'Lady,' he said, 'don't you get upset. Sometimes a man says things he don't mean. I don't reckon he meant to talk to you thataway.' " Later, when Bailey is sent off to his death and the Grandmother calls after him, she finds herself not actually looking at her son but rather at the one who orders the execution. Finally, The Misfit puts on the dead man's blue parrot shirt, and in so doing appropriates the only physical detail we have been given thus far about Bailey's appearance. Although the Grandmother "couldn't name what the shirt reminded her of," The Misfit's putting it on prepares us for her blurring of distinctions between killer and kin that occurs at the story's climax.

Both the talk about Jesus and the confusion of The Misfit with Bailey precipitate the crisis that brings the story rapidly to its conclusion. While the Grandmother passes into a delirium, we watch as The Misfit becomes more and more agitated over a savior he will not believe in because he was not "there" to know for sure. It is precisely at the point when the two seem most profoundly separate from one another that his first show of vulnerability brings them violently together.

> His voice seemed about to crack and the Grandmother's head cleared for an instant. She saw the man's face twisted close to her own as if he were going to cry and she murmured, 'Why, you're one of my babies. You're one of my own children!'

> She reached out and touched him on the shoulder. The Misfit sprang back as if a snake had bitten him and shot her three times through the chest. Then he put his gun down on the ground and took off his glasses and began to clean them.
>
> Hiram and Bobby Lee returned from the woods and stood over the ditch, looking down at the Grandmother who half sat and half lay in a puddle of blood with her legs crossed under her like a child's and her face smiling up at the cloudless sky.
>
> Without his glasses, The Misfit's eyes were red-rimmed and pale and defenseless looking. 'Take her off and throw her where you thrown the others,' he said, picking up the cat that was rubbing itself against his leg.
>
> "She was a talker, wasn't she?" Bobby Lee said, sliding down the ditch with a yodel.
>
> "She would have been a good woman," The Misfit said, "if it had been somebody there to shoot her every minute of her life."
>
> "Some fun!" Bobby Lee said.
>
> "Shut up, Bobby Lee," The Misfit said. "It's no real pleasure in life."
>
> (CS 132-3)

Under the terrible pressure of these events, with a strong sun beating down from the cloudless sky, the old woman suddenly breaks — a moment for which the text allows two very different understandings. The first would see it as a breakdown, the disorientation of a person pushed too far, both physically and mentally. Minutes before, after hearing the pistol shots that killed her son, the narrator tells us the Grandmother threw back her head "like a parched old turkey hen crying for water"; here, she looks at The Misfit dressed in Bailey's shirt and allows fantasy to turn him into the family that has just been destroyed. Our last sight of her, childlike and smiling, suggests a break with reality, the madness into which she has fallen.

Another possible reading, however, would see this not as a breakdown, but as a breakthrough; it would take the narrator's statement that "her head cleared for an instant" not as irony, but as a statement of fact. To be sure, normal reality has collapsed under abnormal circumstances, but this has not been a move into madness. Rather, it affords a moment of insight in which the Grandmother finds in The Misfit's anguished face not a murderous enemy, but a beloved child: "Why you're one of my babies. You're one of my own children!" She has spoken of family and blood before — "You don't look a bit like common blood. I know you must come from nice people!" — but it has been only hypocritical smooth-talk designed to win him over. This is something else, an act of love that reaches toward The Misfit in his distress as if he were one of her "connections" and not the destroyer of them, as if nothing that he had done mattered at all in the face of this transcendent tenderness, smiling up at him even from death.

But if the Grandmother's gesture permits this ambiguity of intepretation, so too does the reaction of The Misfit. On the one hand, we can understand that his violent response to her touch is a response to her violation of that necessary distance between captor and captive, a trespass of a boundary that perhaps threatens him with the possibility of a human relationship that is utterly inadmissible. He can be no mother's son, least of all this one's. His recoil at her touch, "as if a snake had bitten him," restores his inviolability, as well as the isolation which his identity as The Misfit absolutely requires. His statement that she would have been a good woman if someone had held a gun to her head every minute of her life is bitterly ironic when goodness here actually means madness. And yet irony aside, the incident has shaken him to the point that while life before now held no pleasure but meanness, now it holds no pleasure at all. He has reasserted his control but lost any joy in its exercise. To this extent, then, the Grandmother's reaching out has humanized him.

The second reading of The Misfit's reaction would depart from the first primarily by extending it backwards into the story, because it understands both the Grandmother's gesture and The Misfit's reaction to it in terms of the religious dialogue that has gone on between them earlier. She has told him to ask Jesus for help; The Misfit has refused, knowing that to ask for it would ultimately mean having to throw everything away and follow Him. Therefore, when the Grandmother moves out in inexplicable compassion toward him, the threat she poses is not as a crazy woman nor even as a prisoner whose blessing of her persecutor violates all the rules; it is a sign of "what thrown everything off balance" in the first place. He pulls back from what she offers as if it were a deadly snake because he senses that to allow it to strike would, in fact, mean death to his life as The Misfit.

These two readings of the climactic moment in "A Good Man Is Hard To Find" are, quite obviously, on something like the order of nature and grace respectively. While each one is plausible, neither is without its hermeneutical problems. The first stays within a largely psychological frame of reference comfortable to the secular reader because it answers to a "normal" view of the way people work, even under such extreme circumstances as those portrayed here. In other words, the delirious Grandmother confuses Bailey's killer with Bailey, and for this mistake he shoots her, though not without himself being disturbed by the terrible humanity her mad gesture of compassion has exposed him to. But this does not take into account either the conversation about Jesus that preoccupies the whole latter part of the story or the narrator's straightforward introduction of the old woman's move — "the Grandmother's head cleared for an instant." In other words, a strictly naturalistic reading of the story does not deal with all that is there; it seems incomplete because of what it omits from consideration.

But while the second approach to the text makes use of its entirety, and therefore offers itself as a fuller and more satisfying interpretation, it presupposes a rather great deal. In the first place, it asks you to assume that the particular events of the narrative are part of a larger drama of grace into which its participants are irresistibly drawn, not by coincidence or fate, but by God — actors as ill-equipped for their ultimate role as the Grandmother, or as dead set against it as The Misfit. This approach asks you to see them each as one another's divinely-appointed judge, so that while he sentences her to her moment of self-transcendent goodness, she sentences him to a lifetime without pleasure in meanness. Furthermore, it presupposes that the truest understanding of individual or act is not psychological but religious, so that the Grandmother's reaching out to the killer, if irrational, is *above* reason, the revelation of something she participates in, even if it is quite beyond the character we have known thus far. In fact, one might go so far as to say that her inexplicable love for him makes sense only as an expression of God's inexplicable love for us.

This understanding is, of course, very like the one which O'Connor wanted the reader to come away with. We know this for a fact from the remarks she used to preface at least one public reading of the story: "[The Grandmother's] head clears for an instant and she realizes, even in her limited way, that she is responsible for the man before her and joined to him by the ties of kinship which have their roots deep in the mystery she has been prattling about so far."[8] But it is also clear that she made these very explicit remarks in the first place because her experience with readers led her to expect that they would not come up with such conclusions on their own.

From asides in her preface to the story, as well as from her letters to people who made inquiries about its meaning, it is painfully obvious that many of them did not. They thought the Grandmother a witch, or The Misfit a satanic hero, or the latter half of the story a dream in Bailey's mind, or the whole business (as *Time* put it) "witheringly sarcastic." There were not many eyes sharp enough for what she called "the almost imperceptible intrusions of grace," or for "the nature of the violence which precedes and follows them" (M 112).

Today, with both O'Connor's work and her views quite readily available, it is unusual to find readers so far afield from her intentions. Indeed, O'Connor criticism tends to be overly reverential toward her point of view, with her nonfictional writing used to gloss the novels and stories, or to provoke religious readings of her texts that are unwarranted by them.[9] But without O'Connor's interpretation of "A Good Man Is Hard To Find," does the story itself make such a reading compelling? Or, to put it another way, does she leave her agnostic readers so unfulfilled by the naturalistic level on which the story can be read that they nonetheless seek out an interpretation that is alien to them?

Certainly the story employs almost every strategy in O'Connor's book to accomplish this end. To begin with, the Southern setting allows Jesus to be a plausible frame of reference for characters as diverse in type as the Grandmother and The Misfit, and therefore for the reader who vicariously shares their experience. Secondly, the whole structure of the story is streamlined toward a momentous encounter between these two characters, suggesting that their meeting has an ineluctable purpose to it, an all-important meaning that exceeds their understanding of it. This momentousness is heightened by the story's use of violence, which abruptly changes the humorous tone of the first half and forces us to understand that what transpires between these characters is ultimately decisive for them, that "something is going on here that counts." Finally, there is the voice of the narrator which clues our response to the Grandmother's solicitude by telling us what we could not otherwise have known — her "head cleared for an instant" — and thereby makes us unsatisfied with any understanding of her act that does not judge it intentional, sane, and expressive of some new insight.

Nevertheless, even with all these stops pulled, the mystery which the storyteller wants to tell remains mystifying for anyone who is not steeped in O'Connor's world. While undoubtedly more than a mere account of a family murdered on their way to Florida, it is the question of *how much more* that remains open, depending in part on the degree to which the reader shares what we have identified above as the unspoken assumptions of the story. For while the text prepares the reader to accept its events as important, as matters of life and death, it is less clear whether it provides enough to infer the specifically religious importance O'Connor intends. She is interested in drawing lines of spiritual motion, invisible save for the effects of their movement in word, gesture, or event. But such effects remain inscrutable, or are misinterpreted, unless the writer can establish a context for their discernment. It is all very well for her to tell her audience, "You should be on the lookout for such things as the action of grace in the Grandmother's soul, and not for the dead bodies" (M 113). "Such things," however, need to be intelligible in the first place. You cannot see what you do not know.

What we end up with here is the same gap between writer and reader which claimed our attention at the outset of this chapter and which, as we have seen, preoccupied O'Connor throughout her career. Striving at once for clarity and mystery — caught between the need to state and the desire to suggest — her work exemplifies the seemingly insoluble problems of communication faced by a contemporary Christian writer before an unbelieving audience. The surprising extent to which she has been acclaimed in the almost twenty years since her death is a sign of the power of her fiction to override problems it perhaps cannot overcome. It may also show the degree to which familiarity with her thought has instructed us to read her work in her way. In any case, O'Connor provides us with a set of critical terms and fictional strategies that throw light on the work of other laborers in the same vineyard. And it is to the closest of these kin, Walker Percy, that we turn next.

3 Walker Percy

In an article written in the late sixties for the journal of the Committee of Southern Churchmen, Walker Percy reveals much about his own sense of vocation. He compares the serious contemporary novelist, whose concerns are the radical questions of human identity, to the canary that coal miners once took down into the shafts to test the air. "When the canary gets unhappy, utters plaintive cries, and collapses, it may be time for the miners to surface and think things over" (MB 101). The comparison is characteristically humorous and not a little self-deprecating: this kinship with the miner's canary is as close as Percy will come to claiming the role of the prophet. And yet it is precisely as the bearer of urgent Bad News that Percy stakes his claim to our attention, with his insistence that the air is dangerous indeed and a trip above ground the only safe way to figure out why it is getting so difficult to breathe below. Subjected to the same societal pressures that Flannery O'Connor felt and resisted with all her might — pressures to approve the atmosphere, to be positive and even celebratory about the prevailing conditions — Percy takes as his starting point the irrefutable evidence of his own nostrils: *"Something is wrong here; I don't feel good."*

This diagnosis of the contemporary air is made with the precision and scope that marks his peculiar calling, for Percy is a pathologist who has turned his attention from medicine to metaphysics.[1] Beginning with the symptoms of alienation and depression that seem to characterize the post-modern world — as witnessed in the predicament of the man who has solved all his problems but one, how to keep from blowing his brains out — Percy goes on to make an extensive critique of a culture which no longer understands itself, which has no adequate theory of human being and therefore no way of accounting for the prevalence of human alienation. Living as we do at the end of the modern age but before the discovery of that end, our contemporary frame of reference is a strange amalgamation of scientific determinism on the one hand and the ethical remains of Christendom on the other. Within such a framework we are "organisms" supposedly endowed with inalienable rights. We speak of "needs" and "drives" capable of objective satisfaction, but also about the sacred worth of the individual, as if these two worlds of discourse could cohabit without contradiction.

If this amalgam represents the wisdom of the age, it does not offer us any coherent understanding of human beings. Rather, it is a "kind of mishmash view of man, a slap-up model put together of disparate bits and pieces" (MB 19). Questions of theoretical inadequacy aside, Percy's primary concern is that the mishmash has dire consequences for the persons who conceive themselves accordingly. The world it describes is ultimately uninhabitable, pulled apart at the seams by its own contradictions. How, after all, can an "organism" be of sacred worth? How can the ghost inhabit the machine except as a manner of speaking — an attempt to humanize the biological works by means of a nod to that old fiction of Judeo-Christianity, the soul? In Percy's estimate the center does not hold. What we are left with is a world described in *Love in the Ruins* as "broken, sundered, busted down the middle, self ripped from self and man pasted back together as mythical monster, half angel, half beast, but no man" (LR 382-3).

In that same novel Percy goes on to offer us, in lapidary form, his own understanding of human nature, the healthy obverse of the diseased monster, "which is to say sovereign wayfarer, lordly exile, worker and waiter and watcher." What informs both his diagnosis of our sickness and his prescription for our health is an orthodox Roman Catholicism, a belief (to use his inimitable shorthand) in "that unique Thing, the Jewish-People-Jesus-Christ-Catholic-Church" (MB 140). Christianity provides for him a cogent understanding not only of human beings, but of the alienation that seems to poison the contemporary air we breathe. It presents our existence not as "the transaction of a higher organism satisfying this or that need from its environment, by being 'creative' or enjoying 'meaningful relationships,' but as the journey of a wayfarer along life's way" (MB 24). But of course this anthropology of human pilgrimage, of persons truly at home in this world only as long as they remember that they are not entirely of it, makes sense only in the context of a larger understanding of life, in terms of a biblical vision that Percy summarizes with brilliant concision as

> the belief that man was created in the image of God with an immortal soul, that he occupied a place in nature somewhere between the beasts and the angels, that he suffered an aboriginal catastrophe, the Fall, in consequence of which he lost his way and, unlike the beasts, became capable of sin and thereafter became a pilgrim or seeker of his own salvation, and that the clue and sign of his salvation was to be found not in science or philosophy but in the news of an actual historical event involving a people, a person, and an institution.
>
> (MB 18)

Percy has made it clear that his vocation as a Christian novelist is not to preach the gospel, but rather to allow it to be central to his fiction, to color the ultimate concerns that are the burden of his work. And yet to write as such a novelist, from such a standpoint, is also (as we have seen in the preceding chapter) to write from a perspective that is not currently shared by a wide reading audience. It is to speak without consensus. But while Percy holds this problem in common with O'Connor, his profound fascination with the mysterious transaction of language has enabled him to penetrate more deeply into the nature of the "communication event," and also into its failure, than she was able to go. Indeed, one might even claim that the breakdown in understanding, between persons as well as between human and divine, is the abiding subject of his work, the "ruins" out of which both his essays and his novels have grown.

Percy accounts for the present deafness to the gospel in several ways. To begin with, there is what he speaks of as the devaluation of Christian vocabulary: "The old words of grace are worn smooth as poker chips and a certain devaluation has occurred, like a poker chip after it has been cashed in" (MB 116). Far from being lost outright — O'Connor's primary cause for lament — the old, old story, Percy goes on to suggest in the same essay, is now too *familiar* to be heard, "the weariest canned spot announcement on radio/TV, more commonplace than the Exxon commercial." The gospel has become like a word repeated in rapid, mindless succession; it no longer means anything, having fallen victim to its own inflation or become unrecognizably blurred through inferior reproduction. Thus he describes the Christian novelist as "a starving Confederate soldier who finds a hundred-dollar bill on the streets of Atlanta, only to discover that everyone is a millionaire and the grocers won't take the money."

In addition to this devaluation of Christian language, there has also been a disenchantment with the speaker, that is, with the Church. Percy's indictment here is of the moral bankruptcy of Christendom, its capitulation to the secular powers that be and, therefore, its silence about the abuses of those powers: "It is the churches which, far from fighting the good fight against man's inhumanity to man, have sanctified and perpetuated [our] indifference" (MB 117). No person of integrity will listen to a speaker who is morally impoverished; his or her words are not to be trusted, let alone believed. Therefore, as Will Barrett says in *The Second Coming,* perhaps with a glance at the most recent best-seller in American religion, "If the born again are the twice born, I'm holding out for the third go-around" (SC 272).

More serious than either of these obstacles to genuine communication, however, is the possibility that there has been a psychological transformation of humanity that surpasses even the technological revolution in import, a restructuring of human consciousness that will no longer allow people to take account of the Good News. Percy attributes this change in sensibility not to science itself, but to its magical aura, the full sway of the objective-empirical over every sector of reality. The seduction of the layman by this "all-transcending objective consciousness" not only makes it impossible to believe in the reality of what cannot be seen or quantified; it also prevents admittance to one's own subjectivity, to the authority of one's own individual experience, to those deep-seated longings that do not correspond to what the prevailing consensus psychology regards as a legitimate human need. According to Percy, this loss of the Creator has also entailed a loss for the creature, a disinheritance of our full humanity.[2] Because we have historically experienced this double deprivation, it is extremely difficult for the contemporary sensibility to make a recovery. For by eliminating the individual's hunger and thirst for God from the realm of serious consideration, the objective-empirical has effectively precluded the only way that God can be known — in the human need for what transcends the powers of human fulfillment.

And yet if the spirit of the age has built us a perfect house, the best of all possible environments, there remains the non-negotiable fact that the inhabitants walk its halls like spectres of themselves, oppressed by dread, boredom, or the uneasy suspicion that there must be *something* more. The machine may have convinced us that there is no ghost in its works, but nonetheless it continues to be haunted and the technical manuals offer no clue whatsoever to what is actually wrong. It is only then, with the gears grinding or the perfect hum of the machinery no longer bearable, that a person may develop a nose for trouble tantamount to the canary's signalling that something is radically amiss. In this way a recognition of Bad News is both the beginning of wisdom and the growth of a capacity to hear news of any kind, a small but decisive break in the hold of the objective-empirical upon a person's consciousness.

Percy's understanding of his own vocation, then, is not the preaching of the gospel, but the development of the reader's capacity to receive urgent news. His career as a writer began with the publication of a series of essays which directly confront the complexities of such communication: the mystery of words spoken, understood, and acted upon. Although the impulse of the essayist continues, and indeed openly manifests itself not only in nonfictional writing but in frequent philosophical and theological discussion within the novels, Percy has chosen primarily to work in the more indirect mode of fiction; that is, to communicate through story rather than through analyses of the "communication event." One can see this shift as the result of a desire for contact with a larger audience than the readership of *Thought* or *The Modern Schoolman* would afford. More importantly, it represents a different relationship not only with the reader, but with his own ideas and passions. For however rich in parable and illustration the essay form can be — and Percy's are treasure troves of both — the essay's primary goal is to clarify and simplify, to take the wealth of individual instances and form general statements about them. The task of fiction, on the other hand, is to make complicated and concrete. Unlike either the essayist or the scientist, the writer of fiction deals with the specific first and last, the densely particularized life of this or that person. For this reason it is the responsibility of the novelist, as Percy says, "to be chary of categories and rather to focus upon the mystery, the paradox, the *openness* of an individual human existence" (MB 108).

In doing so, of course, the novelist flies in the face of the scientific approach to human existence, which addresses the individual only as "an organism among organisms" (MB 19), as he or she resembles other individuals and conforms to a general theory of behavior. Deliberately working against that grain, Percy's fiction attempts to undo the packaging that has come to enclose and dominate our experience of life. By intensely imagining one person's predicament, he offers us a particularized experience and not some abstract case about whom the social scientist (or essayist) can make generalizations. Percy's hope is that absorption in the vividly related situation of an engaging character may very well lead the reader away from an objective consideration of ideas "out there," and into the concrete realities of his or her own life. The turn to fiction, then, is an attempt to seize the attention of the reader at a deeply imaginative and vulnerable level of consciousness, not primarily to instruct, but rather to engage in a process of discovery, a reclamation of the sovereign self which may as well become the rediscovery of God. To Percy's way of thinking, the story of a man who "comes to himself" stands a better chance to become a catalyst for the reader's own awakening than does an objective study of that phenomenon.

As a specifically Christian novelist, burdened with a discredited Christendom and a religious vocabulary no longer compelling, Percy identifies himself on a number of occasions with the artistry (and the struggle) of Flannery O'Connor. Like her he is willing to use every trick he can think of to catch the reader's attention: "You want to *show* him something, *tell* him something: show and tell!"[3] Elsewhere he lays claim to O'Connor's characteristic strategies of "violence, shock, comedy, insult, the bizarre" as the everyday tools of his trade:

> How could it be otherwise? How else can one possibly write of a baptism as an event of immense significance when baptism is already accepted but accepted by and large as a minor tribal rite somewhat secondary to taking the kids to see Santa at the department store? Flannery O'Connor conveyed baptism through its exaggeration, in one novel as a violent death by drowning. In answer to a question about why she created such bizarre characters, she replied that for the near-blind you have to draw very large, simple characters.
>
> (MB 118)

This quotation, with its allusions both to an O'Connor novel *(The Violent Bear It Away)* and to one of her seminal essays ("The Fiction Writer and His Country"), suggests the extent to which Percy knows her work and approves of her attempts to convince the reader that "something is going on here that counts." Oddly enough, this close affinity with O'Connor has been largely unexplored by Percy's critics, whose interest in his relation to other writers has largely focused on the obvious debt to Kierkegaard and the existentialists; that is, to questions of intellectual formation rather than to those of novelistic practice.[4] Although essentially her contemporary, one might well claim that Percy can best be understood in the light of Flannery O'Connor's work, as following her lead as a Southerner and Roman Catholic exploring violence, shock, and bizarre comedy as viable modes of serious Christian communication. But if the two share a common creed, a penchant for certain kinds of literary assault, and the cartoonist's willingness to reduce the complexity of character and situation to the humorous economy of very large and simple caricatures, any real comparison of their work reveals a divergence of vision and technique that heightens the uniqueness of each.

To begin with, there is the matter of their protagonists. How far a cry are Percy's alienated lawyers and alcoholic doctors, wending their calamitous ways across the golf links, from O'Connor's crazed evangelists, complacent farm women, and would-be intellectuals. It is not simply that Percy has chosen first to place the country club at the symbolic center of his fictional world and then to tell the story of bright middle-class men who are for some reason miserable in this presumably best of all possible worlds. It has much more to do with the fact that unlike O'Connor, he has endowed his central characters with an extraordinary range and depth of self-awareness. His heroes are men both obsessed and articulate about their predicament, however helpless they may actually be to alter it. Whereas O'Connor gives us characters who but slenderly know themselves, who act in ignorance or on the intuitive promptings of their "wise blood," Percy's protagonists are relentlessly self-conscious. They come from a class and a world that has been radically affected by psychoanalysis, and there is perhaps no more dramatic way to perceive this gulf between Percy's characters and O'Connor's than simply by attempting to place Hazel Motes or OE Parker on Will Barrett's psychiatrist's couch or in conversation with Tom More's attending physicians. It is certainly not that Percy presents the psychoanalytic mode as a higher or truer level of consciousness. Quite the contrary, it receives its fair share of ridicule in a number of his works, particularly in *The Last Gentleman* and even more so in *Love in the Ruins.* Nonetheless, psychology creates the climate in which his characters live and move and have their being, as well as informing the confessional manner by which they often present themselves to the reader.

Given this kind of protagonist, then, Percy's novels do not represent the enlargement of an omniscient narrator on the experience of persons largely unaware of the drama in which they play a part. Rather, they are the prolix self-revelations of a man who virtually tells his own story, and in three of the five novels does so quite literally through the device of first-person narration. For this reason our relationship with Percy's main characters is far more crucial, as well as more direct, than is the case with O'Connor. Whether or not we actually see through their eyes and think in their terms, as we do in *The Moviegoer, Love in the Ruins*, and *Lancelot*, our experience of the novels is inevitably our experience of their protagonists.

Apart from this different approach to character O'Connor and Percy also treat the social setting of their fiction in dissimilar ways. O'Connor's "realism of distances" pulls our interest into the shadowy *background* of her narrative rather than into the brightly illumined, intensely detailed foreground we find in Percy's work.[5] To be sure, O'Connor is able to suggest a social order in a few masterful strokes of description, whether it be the pecking order of Mrs. McIntyre's hired help in "The Displaced Person" or the hierarchy of the doctor's waiting room in "Revelation." But even when we move from the short stories to the wider scope of her two novels, her artistry always resembles that of the miniaturist: she gives us a small number of figures, the hint of a landscape or room, a significant gesture. The real action of O'Connor's stories, however, takes place outside time and space, in a spiritual dimension that can only be traced in its enigmatic effects on her characters or in the enlargement of her narrator's voice. She continually asks us to look inside the mores of her countryside to discover there the True Country, whose mysterious reality transcends every locale. What this means is that O'Connor's satiric view, with its strong naturalistic bias, is always giving way to another kind of vision. For while her comic presentation of human habits and foibles works to create a world which we can recognize as our own, the real pull of her narrative is toward the unknown and unfamiliar, a region of experience beyond the reach of satire. Thus the Southern cartoonist in O'Connor is disciplined by her strong drive to move through manners to mystery, from the humorous realism of her fictional surfaces to the deadly serious "distances" beyond and within.

Walker Percy, on the other hand, is far more engrossed in the surfaces of his narrative world and with the satiric possibilities those surfaces provide. His interest in the comic survey of a whole social landscape is most obvious in *Love in the Ruins,* with its microcosmic portrait of the "old violent beloved U.S.A." of the late sixties projected into an indeterminate future. But in the other novels as well we are confronted not only with a spoof of the "isms and asms" that presently govern American life, but are also immersed in a swarm of brand names, regional quirks, class distinctions, and physical types. The effect is a panoramic view of America as might be found in a side-show mirror. Rather than seeming like a means to another end, a point of departure, the creation of this panorama appears to be a central and abiding preoccupation of Percy's fiction. It is as if he felt it his vocation to hold this distorting mirror up to nature, but not to let the reader pass through the satiric looking glass into a world of spiritual implication and extension. We never leave the fun house he describes.

It is possible to take Percy's word for it and to see his devotion to the problematic particularities of American time and place as a sign of his "incarnational, historical, predicamental" world view (MB 111). Satire is also a way for the novelist, like the coal miner's canary, to test the air and to give warning of its dangers. Nor should we discount Percy's fascination with what he, an admirer of Gerard Manley Hopkins, might call the "stipple" of our national life, the pied beauty and madness of our social landscape. Like O'Connor's penchant for the grotesque, this kind of comic survey seems also to be quite simply a dimension of Percy's imagination, the way his mind works. In addition to these explanations, however, there is also the fact that satire can serve to alienate the reader from what it is reflecting, from the world and its values that the satiric glass more or less openly distorts. We might speak, therefore, of his realism of "distancing."[6]

A good example of Percy's practice in this regard can be found in the brief description of the Ohioans with whom Will Barrett temporarily takes up in *The Last Gentleman.*

> They all smelled of new wool and Esquire boot polish and were as healthy and handsome as could be. He hadn't been in their company a week before he became one of them: he called a girl named Carol *Kerrell,* said *mear* for mirror, *tock* for talk, *ottombile, stummick,* and asked for *carmel* candy. The consonants snapped around in his throat like a guitar string. In April he went to Fort Lauderdale. In short, he became an Ohioan and for several weeks walked like a cat with his toes pointed in, drank beer, forgot the old honorable quarrels of the South, had not a thought in his head nor a care in the world.
>
> It did not last.
>
> (LG 21)

We see here a version of what O'Connor spoke of as a novelist's *staring.* In her work this intense scrutiny means a wrestling with outward appearances until, like Jacob with the angel, the struggle yields a spiritual depth. This is not the case with Percy; instead he assumes through his protagonist a "Martian view" (MB 11), the quizzical regard of a stranger in a strange land whose extraordinary attention to the surface and style of things not only enables us to visualize them for ourselves, but ends up making their very recognizability seem both odd and ridiculous. By flooding *Kerrell* and her friends with this intense and flattening light, their ordinariness can seem almost surrealistic, as if their Ohio were a bizarre and foreign country. It is most likely that laughter here arises out of the sheer accuracy of the description: the characteristics of appearance, speech, and body language comprise the image of a familiar "type" which, in the distillation of character into caricature, can be immensely amusing. But there is also something abruptly dismissive about the portrayal, because within the narrative the significance of these handsome if mindless kids has exclusively to do with Will Barrett's absorption in them, with his momentary conviction that they, in their unreflective submersion in a way of life, somehow understand what life itself is all about. In themselves they mean nothing; they have no depths to penetrate. Rather, like so many of the supporting cast among whom Percy places his protagonists, the Ohioans are conjured up only as a comic example of a route the hero cannot go. They constitute a two-dimensional surface intended to dramatize, by contrast, the hero's depth. What we see of them and their world is usually all there is to get — something to laugh at and turn away from.

This kind of satirical representation of society runs the risk of alienating the reader by what may seem, over the long course of a novel, to be a systematic devaluation of the ordinary world, a trivialization of anyone not involved in psychological angst or spiritual quest. This may account for why an otherwise enthusiastic *New York Times* review of *The Second Coming* should charge Percy with having an "impatience with the quotidien" and a "disdain for the everyday."[7] What Percy is counting on, however, is that a humorous distancing from the normal will serve to unite the reader with the protagonist in that character's sense of disorientation and malaise, so that he or she will begin to stare at the assumptions of contemporary life as if they could no longer simply be taken for granted — as if, just possibly, the assumptions of our everyday life were crazy. For unless he works some initial disenchantment with the status quo, some uneasiness with the way things are (however exaggerated the fictional representation), there is no cause for the reader to see the reason or feel the need to look elsewhere. There is no cause, in other words, for the reader to follow the protagonist on his search for another way to live.

What I am suggesting here is that this alienation from what is supposed to be home territory, this estrangement from "Ohio," not only has an important impact on the reader, but that it is an intended (if problematic) feature of Percy's strategy as a religious novelist. For the realization that one may not truly belong to the world in which one lives, any more than the protagonist fits in to the world of the narrative, is the first step in that process of transformation that he speaks of as coming to oneself. Therefore Percy gives us comic distortions of a world clearly recognizable as our own, as if by then rendering it absurd he can break the hold of the present age upon the reader, thereby opening him or her to what may very well be a totally alien point of view: the Christian faith. This is certainly not to maintain that the protagonist's coming to himself always entails a religious conversion, which the reader is then also expected to undergo. The heroes of *The Moviegoer* and *The Last Gentleman* remain very much on an open search, despite the different degrees of Catholic "witness" in each novel, while *Lancelot* tells the story of one man's journey in quite the opposite direction, away from God and toward the Devil. Nonetheless, whether through or in spite of his protagonist, Percy is always prompting the reader to reflect that something is wrong, something is missing, and, moreover, that "the unique Thing, Jewish-People-Jesus-Christ-Catholic-Church" may possibly be the very something waited and watched for.

What I am speaking of here as Percy's prompting of the reader is very different from O'Connor's introduction of the "added dimension." He does not rely on the enlargement of the narratorial voice, on biblical allusion, or on the lyric elevation that usually accompanies O'Connor's epiphanic moments. Instead Percy seems again and again to build into the structure of his narrative two discrete (though often interwoven) situations, each of which represents a different stage of awareness and a different kind of grace. We can identify them succinctly as the experience of catastophe and the receiving of the Christian message — the coming to oneself and the coming into contact with the teachings of the Church. While it is true that for Percy the ability to hear the Good News presupposes the ability to hear news of any kind — that is, presupposes the alertness of characters who have been brought to their senses in some dramatic way, most often by an encounter with death — the novels do not show such protagonists moving from A to B in any programmatic fashion. Indeed, the unique character of each book consists in the way Percy varies his use of these narrative situations, emphasizing catastrophe in *Love in the Ruins* and the delivery of the message in *The Last Gentleman,* or even playing them off against one another in *Lancelot,* where the protagonist comes to himself as a prelude to rejecting the gospel and choosing evil to be his good.

It is also an indication of the unity of Percy's work that what I am calling narrative structures can be explored most directly by turning once again to the essays, where he gives us parables both for the salutary experience of catastophe and for the receiving of Christian news as part of his larger exploration of the "communication event." In the first case, he tells the story of a commuter on the way home from his successful job, a man who inexplicably feels bad in proportion to the many reasons he has to feel good.[8] Suddenly he suffers a severe heart attack and is removed from the train to a station passed countless times but never before visited. When the commuter regains consciousness he is in a strange hospital bed surrounded by unfamiliar people. As his eye wanders around the room, he catches sight of the hand spread out on the sheet in front of him. It is as if he had never seen his own hand until this moment — this extraordinary thing able to move this way and that, to open and close.

Percy goes on to speak about this awakening as a kind of revelation, an experience of what the theologians used to call natural grace. Through the heart attack the commuter was able to encounter things from which he had been abstracted for years, absorbed in "everydayness" as he was. One might even say that the ordeal restored him to himself. The event is of enormous existential importance, for what he chooses to make of the experience will become the whole burden of his future. Whatever happens to him, he is now, in the vocabulary of *The Moviegoer,* onto something. By forcibly breaking in upon the nameless despair in which he once rode the train daily, the catastrophe of the heart attack has liberated him from the paralysis of a living death, launching him upon a search whose nature and destination are as yet unknown, but which is his alone to discover.

This story of the commuter, with its presentation of calamity as an occasion for rebirth, is variously presented throughout the fiction. It recurs when Binx Bolling recalls waking up on a Korean battlefield, when Tom More evades the sniper's bullets, and when Will Barrett finds the will to live once it seems he will be left alone to die. Percy will even return to the detail of the commuter's fascination with his own hand when Lancelot Lamar is shocked into self-awareness after the discovery of his wife's infidelity: "My hands were open in front of my face. The fingers closed and opened. I felt like Rip Van Winkle waking up and testing his bones. Was anything broken? Was I still in one piece?" (LC 201)

"Like Rip Van Winkle waking up." Percy presents the

experience of catastrophe as a rough shaking out of sleep, a blast of cold air, or, as *The Moviegoer* would have it, "a good kick in the ass." Furthermore, it is usually only the reality of death that is powerful enough to quicken people out of the torpor of everyday life and into some kind of active search for what life itself is really about. For this reason Percy plunges his heroes into disaster and ordeal, only to have them speak out of the whirlwind (in words that more or less directly echo the essays) about the worst of times being the best of times, about the preferability of hurricanes over so-called good weather, about the willing return of soldiers to the scenes of their worst nightmares. One might well remark that the uses of adversity are sweet only for the survivors. But Percy's interests are always focused on his protagonist, and therefore on persons who not only live through the experience of catastrophe but discover in the course of it the freedom to act and be. It is as if the necessity to struggle with something outside themselves releases an enormous and purposeful energy, a magnitude of self, that enables them to shake loose of the anxiety and abstraction in which they once lived. What invariably follows is Will Barrett's realization in *The Second Coming* that "all you need to do anything is time to do it, being let alone long enough to do it and a center to do it from" (SC 58). Catastrophe returns Percy's heroes to that central point.

With the notable exception of Lancelot, whose awakening leads him straight into the heart of darkness, Percy's protagonists usually pass through their ordeal to a renewed life in the ordinary world, although an ordinary world cleansed of the deadening effects of "everydayness." Thus *The Moviegoer, Love in the Ruins,* and *The Second Coming* all end with their heroes settled in work, relationship, and domesticity; it is an end to which Lancelot and the Will Barrett of *The Last Gentleman* also aspire but which, for different reasons, they are by no means ready to attain. The sense of mastery which these characters grow toward — the self they come to — enables them to work and marry and be outwardly indistinguishable from anyone else on the five-fifteen commuter train. They seem, in Wallace Stevens' phrase, to live like "Danes in Denmark all day long."

Such appearances are deceiving, however, for the search which catastrophe enables them to begin does not end once they have reached a modicum of psychological health and a bourgeois life-style to go along with it. Once inside their own skins they are able to see without the cloud of anxiety what had been so obscurely terrifying before: the fact that they do not belong to this world, even though they can finally live happily within it; that their needs can never be completely "satisfied" even when they seem to be completely met; that Denmark is not, in fact, their native land. For it is only in the process of becoming in some way "sovereign" or "lordly" that they can learn the deeper truth of their wandering and exile, their profound need to keep on searching for something more. Thus, to use Percy's own typology, his fiction variously presents us with a Rip Van Winkle who, once awakened by disaster, discovers himself to be a Robinson Crusoe. He is not a man at home after a twenty year nap, but a castaway combing a foreign beach for clues, scanning the sea, yearning for news of home.

If this yearning is a kind of natural revelation that comes as a result of catastrophe, the news of home is another mattery entirely. It is a revelation of the supernatural, the discovery that the hero's nameless and open search is tied to what Val Sutter in *The Last Gentleman* describes as "the whole business: God, the Jews, Christ, the Church, grace, and the forgiveness of sins" (LG 301). This brings us to the second of the two deep structures within Percy's fiction, the deliverance of Christian news to one who has been awakened to hear it. And once again a parable from the essays provides our point of entry into the varied practice of the novels. In "The Message in the Bottle," the title piece of that collection, Percy describes a castaway who has lost everything, even his memory, in a shipwreck. When he regains consciousness he discovers himself on a populated island, among whose people he soon makes his way and his home. He becomes, as we say, a useful member of that society, but perhaps out of an old sense of loss he takes to walking the beach in the mornings. On those walks he regularly finds tightly corked bottles, each of which contains a different message. Some of them are statements of knowledge whose truth can be demonstrated by anyone on the island at any time, such as "Water boils at 100 degrees at sea level." Others express a particular event or state of affairs that is of special, even urgent relevance to the one who reads them: "There is fresh water in the next cove." Percy calls these latter statements "news." The special difference between the two messages has to do with the situation of the man who uncorks the bottle, whether he wants to know something about water, as a piece of knowledge *sub specie aeternitatis*, or whether he is dying of thirst.

But even in the matter of news alone, the messages fall into two kinds. There are those which convey island news pertinent to the life of anyone who lives there. The whereabouts of fresh water clearly falls into this category. Such news does not entirely satisfy the castaway, however, for the simple reason that he is a castaway and therefore wants very much to know about life off the island — the world which he cannot remember, but which he also cannot help but miss, no matter how good things are where he lives now. Therefore the messages he most craves are those which bring him news from across the sea. Neither island knowledge nor island news can be fully relevant to the predicament of a castaway, for nothing "here" can tell him where he comes from or who he really is.

For Percy, who follows his Heideggerian parable with an interpretation of it, this news from across the sea is nothing other than the Christian gospel. What it tells cannot be deduced or discovered anywhere on the island world of human existence, but must be delivered from someplace else: it is *revealed* news. This is true even though the news speaks very much to the condition of island life and is, so to speak, about the Life of the island. Furthermore, what distinguishes it from every other message is the impossibility of communicating it in a bottle; this is a piece of news that can only come from hearing. It is the story of a Person to be told by one person to another. The newsbearer has been empowered by an authority that has come from the outside; the ability to speak it is not a talent, let alone anything like a skill to be acquired. And while the message delivered cannot be validated by the one who receives it, anymore than the newsbearer's credentials can ever be fully checked, what the hearer has to go on is the gravity of the news, the sober perseverance of the one who braves the seas to bring it, and the crucial fact that the castaway needs what he hears: news of where he came from, and who he is, and what he must do.

At the very end of the essay Percy asks what will happen to the one who listens to such a messenger, only to immediately answer his own question with the final sentence of the piece: "Well then, the castaway will, by the grace of God, believe him" (MB 149). The statement makes an extremely bold claim, but one which is carefully qualified by the notion of God's grace — that is, by the introduction of the unknown and unaccountable. In matters of belief there can be, of course, no *quid pro quo*, no automatic assumption that believing will follow upon hearing, no matter how "lively" the telling may be. All the messenger can do is pass on what has been received; the rest is a mystery hidden in the freedom of the one who hears.

Percy presents this encounter and this mystery in different ways throughout his fiction. Sometimes the coming of the message has sudden and dramatic impact, as when a person in distress hears the call, Come! and heeds it. In *The Last Gentleman* Val Sutter describes precisely this situation when she recalls a life-transforming conversation with the nun who silently shared her library carrel for an entire academic year and then broke that silence with a question:

> "She said, what's the matter with you? I said, what do you mean what's the matter with me? She said, you look half dead. . . . I said Yes, I am half dead. She said why? I said I don't know. She said how would you like to be alive? I said I'd like that. She said all right, come with me. That was it. . . . I received instruction, made a general confession, was shriven, baptized, confirmed and made my first vows [as a nun] all in the space of six weeks. They thought I was crazy. . . . When all I'd done was taken them at their word."[9]

While it might be assumed that the speaker here has reduced a complex exchange to its most rudimentary elements, I think on the contrary that Percy intends us to take these few words, and Val's overwhelming response to them, as paradigmatic of castaway conversation: stark, direct, the voice of authority spoken directly to human need. There is no desire for spiritual analysis here; rather, Percy wants to highlight how one can, by God's grace, believe the newsbearer straightaway and then act on what one hears. Complexity of motive, ambivalence, personal history, and every other possible consideration are brushed aside before the sheer and surprising fact of Val's willingness to follow.

This taking the newsbearer at his or her word is once again the point of an episode at the end of the novel, when a Roman priest delivers the "truths of religion" to Val's dying brother Jamie, who asks, goggle-eyed at the Good News, why he should believe so extraordinary an account.

> The priest leaned hard on his fists. "It is true because God Himself revealed it as the truth."
>
> Again the youth's lips moved and again the priest turned to the interpreter.
>
> "He asked how, meaning how does he know that?"
>
> The priest sighed. "If it were not true," he said to Jamie, "then I would not be here. That is why I am here, to tell you."
>
> (LG 404)

Even more striking here than in the earlier encounter between Val and the nun is the unadorned proclamation of this messenger. The unnamed priest speaks with utter confidence about an objective truth; he also speaks, though in his own voice and about himself, with the impersonal authority of the Church. Percy heightens our awareness of this authority by eliminating anything even vaguely resembling Christian apologetics: the priest has a message revealed by God and brought by him. There is nothing more to be said. And yet the stark simplicity of this declaration is perhaps easier to entertain in parable than it is in a realistic narrative, where the voice of authority can sound so oppressively authoritarian that one notices the disconcerting fact that the priest's fists are clenched throughout this exchange! To be sure, there are reasons why the delivery of the message should be portrayed in this way. We are, after all, at a death bed, with Jamie barely able to communicate his wishes, let alone discuss the "truths of religion." It is also true that the novel elsewhere provides such discussion through Sutter Vaught and his extraordinary diary. Clearly at this point, however, Percy wants to intensify the drama of a life choice by boiling everything down to the Kierkegaardian essentials, to yes or no, in order that the reader may see, in O'Connor's words, that something is going on here that counts. The problem is whether the reader can make even this leap of faith, can hear the priest tell Jamie, "If it were not true then I would not be here," and find such a statement anything more than a tautology or a parent telling a child, "Do it because I told you to." Of such communication may very well be the kingdom of heaven, but it also runs the risk of discrediting itself by sheer arbitrariness.

Percy did something rather different in his next novel, *Love in the Ruins,* where the priestly representative of Christian orthodoxy does not so much deliver news as reconcile the protagonist to what he already knows. Like the cleric in *The Last Gentleman,* Fr. Smith has all the gestures and stock phrases of his calling. He handles the duties of his vocation with a routine faithfulness that Percy seems always to want to emphasize in his priests, as if to suppress any notion of "originality" in favor of the ordinary obedience of messenger to message. He gives us apostles instead of geniuses, to recall the Kierkegaardian distinction extremely important for Percy.[10] But if Fr. Smith is an ordinary man, we learn from More's recollections of the past how troubled his life has been, first by alcohol, then by occasional trips "to a Gulf Coast home for addled clerics," and finally by a total breakdown. Far from being set apart from the spiritual malaise of others, he has also been, like More, a victim of the contemporary air, a former inmate of the psychiatric ward who baffled his behaviorist examiners with the truth: "I am surrounded by the corpses of souls. We live in a city of the dead" (LR 186). But perhaps because he has known More's own condition firsthand, he is able to present Christianity's comic solution, both to More and to the reader, in a less abstract and seemingly arbitrary manner than the priest in *The Last Gentleman.* The message from across the sea comes from one who has been in the adjacent hospital bed. As wounded healer, he prescribes a cure as one who has himself been stricken with the disease and then delivered from it, thereby serving as an example of how one can live and work in the city of the dead while bearing witness to something more. By having his newsbearer in many ways resemble his castaway, Percy enhances the believability of the messenger and, by extension, of what he bears witness to.

It is not only through nuns and priests, however, that the teachings of the Church explicitly break through the surface of the narrative. In both *The Moviegoer* and *Love in the Ruins* the protagonist is confronted by a child steeped in the orthodoxy and vocabulary of the Baltimore Catechism, whose straightforward and profound faith commands the hero's attention not by virtue of any ecclesiastical authority but because of the physical suffering which they not only endure but transcend. Aside from the close bonds of kinship — Lonnie is Binx Bolling's half-brother, Samantha is More's daughter — these children draw the protagonist to them by the sheer power of their belief, as well as by their great concern for the one who does not believe. Thus Binx Bolling envies Lonnie because "he has the gift of believing that he can offer his sufferings in reparation for men's indifference to the pierced heart of Jesus" (MG 137), deeply touched that as one of those men he is nonetheless the specific person for whom Lonnie makes his communion. But most of all it is the proximity of these children to death that lends them their enormous personal authority and gives an eloquent urgency to their concerns.

> "Just promise me one thing, Papa."
> "What's that?"

> "Don't commit the one sin for which there is no forgiveness."
>
> "Which one is that?"
>
> "The sin against grace. If God gives you the grace to believe in him and you refuse, the sin will not be forgiven you."
>
> "I know." I took her hand, which even then looked soiled and chalk dusted like a schoolgirl's.
>
> (LR 373-4)

As is true of all the Christian truth-tellers in Percy's fiction, Lonnie with his prayers to the pierced heart of Jesus and Samantha with her talk about the unforgivable sin speak an old-fashioned theological language, one that evokes a linguistic and conceptual world far from our culture's psychological jargon or, for that matter, from contemporary religious expression. Such talk cannot help but strike the reader's ear as an anachronism, an arcane and bizarre speech from another age. And yet it may well be Percy's intention to capitalize on the foreignness of its sound, not only to turn attention to a whole new kind of discourse, but to suggest through it another country, a different mind, an unselfconscious assurance on the part of the speaker singularly absent from our "island" communication.

In *Lancelot* Percy does not draw our attention to the newsbearer by curious language, but rather by the curiosity generated by that person's silence. This novel is the record of Lancelot Lamar's unburdening of himself to a childhood friend who has become a priest. But instead of offering counsel, the confessor only listens, allowing Lamar to come to the point at the very end of the novel that he wants to know what the other man is thinking. In answer to Lamar's question, "Is there anything you want to tell me," he replies, "Yes," and with that single word concludes the novel, a striking contrast to the hateful negation that has spewed forth from this most problematic of Percy's protagonists. We do not know what the priest might go on to say, but there is the possibility that Lancelot will be able to hear his words, that the torrent of his own speech has been a preparation for this moment of listening, even though what is to follow will come from a man whose life it is to love the world that Lancelot hates, to "preach the gospel, turn bread into flesh, forgive the sins of Buick dealers, administer communion to suburban housewives" (LC 256). As Percy writes in an essay, "In such times, when everyone is saying 'Come!' it may well be that the best way to say 'Come!' is to remain silent" (MB 148). *Lancelot* presents that possibility.

Given this tendency to repeatedly play variations on his own themes, it comes as no surprise that in his most recent novel, *The Second Coming,* Percy should once again turn to the communication event that takes place between newsbearer and castaway, or that his latest version of it should combine elements of the earlier treatments we have just surveyed. The climactic moment in question takes place at the very end of the novel, but in retrospect we can see that it has been prepared for from the beginning, even before the opening line, by the book's title. The phrase "second coming" refers in one sense, of course, to the return of Will Barrett, along with a number of other characters and story lines, from *The Last Gentleman,* which takes place thirty or so years before the present action. But more importantly it announces from the outset the eschatological obsession that drives Will Barrett throughout the book, an obsession with the possibility that the Jews are returning to the Holy Land in preparation for Christ's second coming and, therefore, that "God's plan is working out." Thus, the seeker after "something" in *The Last Gentleman* has become by the outset of this novel a genuine, if contentious, seeker after God.

For this reason Barrett is always looking for signs, even to the point, in one of the novel's great moments, of attempting to force God's hand by means of a test, an experiment designed to prove once and for all if He exists: "No more tricks! No more *deus absconditus!* Come out, come out, wherever you are, the game's over" (192). The results, of course, are inconclusive — neither yes nor no, but only a "muddy maybe" — and the questioning continues as before. But even though Barrett lives in "the most Christian town in North Carolina" he cannot find anyone who is able to interpret the signs he himself cannot understand, or to bear witness convincingly to the "plan" he only dimly perceives through the pain of his own history and experience. Surrounded on all sides by belief, there is nonetheless no one for him to believe in.

It is then that he meets Fr. Weatherbee, an eccentric and presumably Episcopal priest who, after fifty years as a missionary to remote parts of the Philippines, is now a senior citizen absorbed in the labyrinth of model trains that fill the attic of the St. Mark's nursing home. According to Jack Curl, the new-breed chaplain of the home who has nervously deflected all Barrett's religious questions with invitations to ecumenical "weekends with God in a wonderful setting," Fr. Weatherbee has two all-consuming beliefs: the Seaboard Air Line Rail Road and the apostolic succession. When Barrett asks about the latter, Curl gives him an ironically-delivered definition ("A laying on of hands which goes back to the Apostles"), which the old man immediately follows by a terse and unambiguous claim ("It happened."). Weatherbee's voice is dry and hoarse, his demeanor ridiculous, but his words have a ring of authority to them that is striking, especially in contrast to Jack Curl's arch vacuity. He *knows* what he believes.

Because Barrett recognizes this, he returns to the old priest at the end of the novel. In one respect this is part of his larger plan to foster the "second coming" of a number of nursing home inmates, but in this case he has a pressing and personal request: he wants Fr. Weatherbee to marry him to Allison Huger, the woman with whom he has, quite literally, fallen in love. Weatherbee quickly suggests that Jack Curl is the cleric for the job. After so long in the Philippines, he is baffled by the "madness of the new church, the madness of America, and telling one from the other," but Barrett will have none of the other priest. He knows that anyone who takes the apostolic succession seriously must also believe in signs, and if in signs then in the divine plan that Barrett wants to know even if he cannot yet believe in it:

> "Excuse me, Father, please bear with me a moment." (Father? Perhaps he didn't like to be called Father? Reverend? Mister? Sir?) "What I am suggesting is that though I am an unbeliever, it does not follow that your belief, the belief of the church, is untrue, that in fact it may be true, and if it is, the Jews may be the clue. Doesn't Scripture tell us that salvation comes from the Jews? At any rate, the Jews are the common denominator between us. That is to say, I am not a believer but I believe I am on the track of something. I may also tell you that I have the gift of discerning people and can tell when they know something I do not know. Accordingly, I am willing to be told whatever it is you seem to know and I will carefully attend to what you say. It is on these grounds that I ask you to perform the ceremony. In fact, I demand it — ha ha — if that is what it takes. You can't turn down a penitent, can you? We are also willing to take instructions, as long as you recognize that I cannot and will not accept all of your dogmas. Unless of course you have the authority to tell me something I don't know. Do you?" (358)

There is a strangely familiar ring to this declaration that the hero is "on the track of something," with its comic asides lightening the somewhat ponderous tone of a lawyer talking to a jury. It is almost as if we can hear in Barrett's speech the voices of other Percy protagonists and the concerns of earlier Percy essays. Within the narrative, however, Fr. Weatherbee's response is a troubled, "Oh dear." He does not want to deliver Christian news to this bizarre man, or have anything to do either with his religious instruction or his wedding. In fact, the demand of this particular zany castaway to be told something he does not know and may not accept is further confirmation of the old man's sense of estrangement from the America in which he finds himself, quite paradoxically, at sea. Why is it, he asks no one in particular, that Americans who are "the best dearest most generous people on earth" are so unhappy? Such questions are music to Will Barrett's ears, but the priest will not pay attention to his renewed chatter about "signs." Instead, he reminisces about the Mindanao villagers he would visit only once every year: a foreign people among whom he felt himself totally welcomed and at home. "They believed me! They believed the Gospel whole and entire, and the teachings of the church. They said that if I told them, then it must be true or I would not have gone to so much trouble. During my absence betrothed couples remained continent and cheerful of their own volition" (359).

Given the actual history of Christian missions, not to mention today's scepticism about poor but happy villagers remaining continent and cheerful of their own volition, it is hard not to dismiss this as an old missionary's fantasy and even more difficult to take it as gospel. And yet allowing for a measure of intentional exaggeration, I think we are meant to take what Fr. Weatherbee says here very seriously, for everything he says — everything Barrett clamors to hear more of — has essentially been written by Percy before. The critique of American unhappiness is pondered in *Love in the Ruins,* as well as in a number of the essays, while the story of the newsbearer who is believed because he has gone to so much trouble to deliver the news is, as we have seen in *The Last Gentleman* and the essay "The Message in the Bottle," a recurring paradigm. Even Fr. Weatherbee's reluctance to answer Barrett's demands, which would seem like the new twist here, recalls Sutter Vaught's treatment of him earlier, in *The Last Gentleman,* as well as the provocative silence of Lancelot's priestly interlocutor.

For anyone who knows Percy's work, in other words, it is impossible to ignore the evidence that the priest is actually the author in comic disguise or to escape the impression that we are being taught an old lesson. Perhaps aware of this, Percy lessens the danger of didacticism by immediately having Fr. Weatherbee retreat into his doddering persona ("If only he could get back to the Atchison, Topeka and the Santa Fe and the lonesome whistle of the Seaboard Air Line") and then by ending the novel with his protagonist's renewed search:

> Will Barrett stopped the old priest at the door and gazed into his face. The bad eye spun and the good eye looked back at him fearfully: What do you want of me? What do I want of him, mused Will Barrett, and suddenly realized he had gripped the old man's wrists as if he were a child. The bones were like dry sticks. He let go and fell back. For some reason the old man did not move but looked at him with a new odd expression. Will Barrett thought about Allie in her greenhouse, her wide gray eyes, her lean muscled boy's arms, her strong quick hands. His heart leaped with secret joy. What is it I want from her and him, he wondered, not only want but must have? Is she a gift and therefore a sign of a giver? Could it be that

> the Lord is here, masquerading behind this simple silly holy face? Am I crazy to want both, her and him? No, not want, must have. And will have. (360)

To the question of whether the Lord is masquerading behind Fr. Weatherbee's "simple silly holy face" there is no doubt but that Percy wants us to say yes. Certainly for Barrett himself the question is a rhetorical one: he knows quite well what he is looking at because he knows what he is looking for. But if we turn our attention from this particular character to the imagined reader, turn from the story of a man looking for the Lord to the experience of a secular person reading about it, the matter becomes far more difficult. We know that Percy is interested in the novel as a means to both challenge the powerful sway of the contemporary age and to open readers to the religious dimension of their own lives. Nonetheless, can a work of fiction unmask God's presence for those not already looking for it? Or, to put it somewhat differently, is there sufficient reason for a reader to take Fr. Weatherbee as seriously as Percy intends?

It does not work to claim that the reader will accept the novelist's "message" because he has gone to so much trouble in writing it and must therefore be telling the truth. Even if one were to accept that such a communication event is actually the way some people come to faith, the fact remains that Percy is not an apostle but a novelist, and as a novelist his only authority is the power of his narrative art. His task then is to suggest the reality of the divine masquerade by creating a fictive world in which signs do have a mysterious significance, in which an engaging plot can maybe lead the reader to entertain, perhaps for the very first time, the larger notion of a plan outside the narrative. The burden of such a writer will be to make religious longing plausible for people who have never admitted such feelings, in hopes that the world of the fiction will be read back into the world of the reader, so that the experience of Will Barrett in *The Second Coming*, for instance, may serve as a new perspective through which to see one's own life in a different way: in radical relationship to God.

This returns us once more to the crucial function of the protagonist in Percy's fiction, for in the absence of a dominant narrator what the novels finally rely on is our strong identification with the hero and our vicarious participation in his search. It is because of this identification with Barrett that Fr. Weatherbee most probably gets his hearing. This is not to discount the possibility that what Percy says through him may have its own powers of persuasion, so that a person in agreement with this particular indictment of America — "How pleasure-loving! How lascivious! Above all, how selfish!" — may very well begin to pay attention to the religious beliefs that ultimately inform it. But it seems to be more likely that the reader stares at this "simple silly holy face" (and attempts to see in it more than meets the eye) because of the fact that Will Barrett is driven to do so.

If this is the case, then Percy's primary concern must inevitably be to make his protagonist as engaging as possible in order to seduce the reader into territory he or she would not otherwise visit. In the figure of Will Barrett he has amassed the appeal of earlier characters: the intelligence and wit, the flights of verbal brilliance, the winning vulnerability, the infectious excitement of a discoverer on the track. Like Tom More, Barrett also has the charm of what R. W. B. Lewis has called the picaresque saint: a character who through his own weakness and suffering participates in our "tragic fellowship," but who is also impelled at any cost to transcend it.[11] Percy knows that the rogue is often able to lead where the holy man can get no one to follow, and so with these protagonists he gives us an orthodox sensibility engulfed in the comic morass of a deranged life — a seeker after righteousness who is not himself righteous, an antic clown who poses only the most serious questions. Thus in *The Second Coming* Barrett functions very much like the spectral presence in one of his own fantasies, the truth seeker who crazily disrupts the platitudes of a Norman Rockwell Thanksgiving dinner with his desperate hunger to know:

> *Where is it? What is missing? Where did it go? I won't have it! I won't have it! Why this sadness here? Don't stand for it! Get up! Leave! Let the boat people sit down! Go live in a cave until you've found the thief who is robbing you. But at least protest. Stop, thief! What is missing? God? Find him!* (273)

The degree to which any given reader identifies with Will Barrett, and therefore with the inner action of the narrative is an individual matter difficult to assess. Certainly one can be moved by the novel to ask Barrett's question, "What is missing?", without having to supply the answer personified by Fr. Weatherbee. "God" can be Barrett's reply and not one's own, for the reader is free to choose even though the novelist's cards are clearly on the table. Where Percy seems to me strangely to work at cross purposes with himself, however, is in tying Barrett's religious longings to his biochemistry. For not only is the "petit-mal temporal lobe epilepsy" caused by pH imbalance the stated reason for his frequent fainting spells, it also radically affects his concern about signs, the Second Coming of Christ, the return of Jews to the Holy Land, and the discernible plan of God. In short, it affects all the preoccupations that have distinguished Barrett throughout the novel and have finally driven him to the confrontation with Fr. Weatherbee. "When his speedy hydrogen ions departed," says the narrator, "so did the Jews" (357). The "objective-empirical" would dismiss Barrett's ultimate concerns as *wahnsinnige*

Sehnsucht, an inappropriate longing caused by petit-mal seizures plus "an unstable pH which fluctuates between a mild alkalosis and acidosis" (303). This dismissal goes against everything that Percy believes to be true about the deepest longing of human nature, and yet it is the narrator who makes the connection between Barrett's physical state and his spiritual search to be a fact of the narrative, and not simply a delusion of science. Therefore he gives us reason to reflect on what he cannot want us to believe, namely, that the divine masquerade behind Fr. Weatherbee's face may be a hallucination caused by the fluctuation of the hydrogen ion.

Despite this confusion, what we are left with at the conclusion of *The Second Coming* is another version of that essential yes which is Percy's essential ending: the affirmation that in coming to oneself one comes to the desire for something more and someone else. For Barrett that someone is greater than the woman he loves; it is the God in whom he cannot yet believe, but whom he "must have. And will have." The fiction of Iris Murdoch is also filled with such longings, as well as with the catastrophes that release and activate them. But for her, as we shall see next, the experience of grace is primarily an event between persons, a mysterious reality that resolutely remains a mystery *not* to be had.

4 Iris Murdoch

In Walker Percy's reflections on the identity of the religious novelist, a category he makes commodious enough to include both Jean-Paul Sartre and Flannery O'Connor, Percy explains his qualifying term in this way. The religious novelist is one who has "explicit and ultimate concern with the nature of man and the nature of the reality where man finds himself" (MB 102). Atheism itself is no bar; all that matters is a passionate conviction about "man's nature, the world, and man's obligation in the world." Percy then goes on to observe that while there are numerous examples of such writers to be found in Russian, French and American literature, writers deeply concerned either with the absence of God or with His troubling presence, the English novelist, so he claims, is not much interested one way or the other.

One hopes that this generalization was not intended to be taken seriously. Certainly it sweeps over much evidence to the contrary, including writers such as Evelyn Waugh, Graham Greene, William Golding, and Anthony Burgess. It is, however, with the example of Iris Murdoch that I want specifically to refute him, not only because her novels show the requisite concern with questions of who we are and what kind of universe we live in, but because like both O'Connor and Percy she too has written extensively in non-fictional prose about the religious crisis of the present time, a time when "Christianity is not abandoned so much as simply unknown. A generation has been growing up outside it."[1]

Murdoch sounds uncannily like Flannery O'Connor in this remark, and yet ironically (given his slur against the English) it is Walker Percy whom she and her career resemble more, moving back and forth as she has done between philosophical analysis and the practice of fiction in an attempt to come to grips with our contemporary spiritual malaise. Thus she writes in her seminal 1961 essay, "Against Dryness," "We live in a scientific and anti-metaphysical age in which the dogmas, images, and precepts of religion have lost much of their power. We have not recovered from two world wars and the experience of Hitler. We are also heirs of the Enlightenment, Romanticism, and the Liberal tradition. These are the elements of our dilemma: whose chief feature, in my view, is that we have been left with far too shallow and flimsy an idea of human personality" (AD 16). Throughout the wide range of her published work — from her Oxford doctoral dissertation (*Sartre: Romantic Rationalist,* 1953) to her most recent (and twentieth) novel, *Nuns and Soldiers* (1980) — Murdoch, no less than Percy, has been preoccupied with religious problems. Such problems include the decay of believed Christianity, the loss of its central authority in western society (either as something adhered to or actively opposed), and the consequent vacuum in our moral, as well as spiritual, lives.

What profoundly separates her from either of the two writers with whom we have been concerned thus far, however, is the fact that she speaks to the issue of lost belief from the other side of the experience. Murdoch is one of those for whom God has died. She takes this demise, as it were, on faith, as an assumption she knows can be challenged. While at times she seems to find this growing consensus about the nonexistence of God to be a liberation or enlargement of human being, her more predominant concern is with the general spiritual impoverishment that has accompanied the waning of religion. With the failure of philosophy and political thought to provide guidance in this regard, she sees us as left standing in need of ways to understand and deepen our experience of man's nature, the world, and man's obligation to the world, to recall Percy's words on the task of the religious novelist. We are in need of a way "to picture, in a non-metaphysical, non-totalitarian, non-religious sense, the transcendence of reality" (AD 19).

What we have in Murdoch, therefore, is not the search for a new language of grace capable of communicating an ancient message to the contemporary reader; we have, rather, the search for an entirely new *concept* of grace, independent of any notion of a gracious God opening our lives to an experience of Himself. Given a world without God, Murdoch wants to discover how men and women can know the transcendence of reality when there is no divinity to pray to for assistance or upon whom to focus one's longing; when instead of God we have only the sense that "there is more than this," that the loving regard of other persons and things is a self-validating experience of goodness whose sovereign value is both the goal and the reward of the spiritual life.

Murdoch's ideas on what she calls the nonreligious transcendence of reality can be readily culled from her philosophical works, especially from the three essays collected under the title *The Sovereignty of Good.* Despite her reluctance to be considered a philosophical novelist, there is an unquestionably close connection between this writing and her fiction. As with Percy, there are times when the difference between them seems not to exist at all, so close can be the voice of character or narrator to the one we have come to know as the author's own. Once again we find a writer implicitly encouraging us to gloss one body of work with another. And yet, however well the elucidation of Murdoch's theory may prepare us to understand what she thinks, and thus help us to recognize some of her intentions for her work, what she actually portrays in the novels is something more rich and complicated, perhaps something even subversive of her attempts to move the reader toward a sense of *nonreligious* transcendence.

This is not simply to say the obvious, that Murdoch's ideas are less clear when embodied and particularized in narrative than when discoursed upon in an essay, for art always enriches issues by confusing them, by making them more opaque and consequently more true to life. It is to suggest, rather, that her fictions are more religiously ambiguous than her stated philosophical position would encourage us to assume, in some cases (especially in her more recent novels) permitting a theological reading as valid as any which fits more comfortably with what we know to be her view of life.

The situation I am describing here is exactly the opposite of what we found in O'Connor, for whereas we were concerned with that author's attempts to surmount the twin problems of over- and understatement in order to convey her Christian vision, we are now interested in the way Murdoch's fiction presents a religious vision which is not one to which she subscribes at all. It is one which she wants, in fact, to transcend and translate into other terms. For while Murdoch has presumably set out to portray a world without God, she has nonetheless, I would argue, written a number of novels in which it seems quite as possible for Him to be in the picture as not. All depends on the disposition of the reader and the way he or she comes over the course of the novel to construe its evidence, to experience its events. Despite what we know from her philosophical writing, despite the frequency with which she shows her authorial hand (and the assumptions that guide it), her fictional attempts at demythologization nonetheless allow the reader to remythologize, to choose whether the world one reads in portrays the absence of God or, on the contrary, the dark mystery of His presence. The freedom of interpretation, and its burden, falls upon the reader.

In turning to Iris Murdoch, therefore, the problems we encounter are a great deal more complex than what we found in O'Connor and Percy, who are Christians concerned to reach the non-Christian with what has become an alien vision no longer capable of being conveyed directly. To be sure, we are still concerned with problems of communication, with the way a writer narrates a "religious" view of life in order that it may take on the compelling force of reality itself. To this end we need to look at Murdoch's beliefs, as well as at the narrative strategies she uses to make her claims upon the reader. But in addition to this we must attend to the puzzling phenomenon of the texts themselves, to the way their strategies often seem to work against their presumed purposes, communicating with great power and eloquence what we otherwise know the author to have discarded. What I want to investigate, then, is the strange possibility that an avowedly non-Christian writer, using Christian language and tradition for her own quite different ends, can produce novels of powerful and genuine Christian interpretation. For it seems to me, especially in her later work, that one is left with the option of seeing that the goodness toward which her characters move (or from which they move away) may actually be God after all. At the very least, the mystery of human life may be a great deal more mysterious in the world of Iris Murdoch's fiction than has been accounted for by her philosophy.

What that philosophy is can be summarized fairly briefly. Dissatisfied with the various notions of human being available to us since World War II, none of which seem to place "man against a background of values, of realities, that transcend him" (AD 18), Murdoch bases her own anthropology on a thoroughly pessimistic assessment of who and what we are. Although no Freudian in any doctrinaire sense, her view of human nature seems to coincide with Freud's doctrine of original sin, summarized by Murdoch in *The Sovereignty of Good* as follows: the individual psyche is "an ego-centric system of quasi-mechanical energy, largely determined by its own individual history, whose natural attachments are sexual, ambiguous, and hard for the subject to understand or control. Introspection reveals only the deep tissue of ambivalent motive, and fantasy is stronger than reason. Objectivity and unselfishness are not natural to human beings" (SG 51). Murdoch considers Freud's pessimism to be a realistic portrayal of what she speaks of as fallen man; like him, she sees us as "benighted creatures sunk in a reality whose nature we are constantly and overwhelmingly tempted to deform by fantasy" (AD 20). It should come as no surprise, then, that the characters who crowd her fiction answer, with a few notable exceptions, so clearly to this description. For underneath their upper middle-class veneer, these sophisticated men and women are ready to transform all of reality into projections of personal wishes and needs, are seldom capable of objectivity or unselfishness, are driven by fantasies "stronger than reason."

In addition to this view of human nature as tirelessly looking after and at itself, there is Murdoch's even more sobering assessment of our existence in the larger scheme of things, when seen against the background of a blind and indifferent universe in which the "fat relentless ego" travels in its own self-preoccupied circles (SG 52). Murdoch assumes that we are what we seem to be, transient mortals subject to both necessity and chance, inhabitants of a world to which there is no point or *telos*, no overarching plan or purpose, no God or godlike substitute, be it Reason or Science or History. "We are simply here," she writes, "and if there is any kind of sense or unity in human life, and the dream of this does not cease to haunt us, it is of some other kind and must be sought within a human experience which has nothing outside itself" (SG 79). The contrast with Walker Percy in this regard is striking, for while Murdoch would agree with him on the Heideggerian premise that we are all of us castaways who are "simply here," the memory of some other home where we truly belong is for her a recurring but nonetheless false dream. She denies the existence of any news from across the sea or an identity that awaits completion only elsewhere. The sole message she recognizes is that which is discovered and conveyed on this island world, within a naked human experience "which has nothing outside itself."

The dream of an "elsewhere," or of a suprapersonal unity of which we are all somehow a constituent part, is in Murdoch's eyes always a false hope, a self-generated consolation through which fantasy transforms the universe into what we would surely prefer it to be — patterned, meaningful, closed and contained, a place where Someone is ultimately in control, a moral order in which there is some extrinsic reason to be good and some reward for being so. Because Christianity has offered western civilization its greatest consolation in all these ways, with its Creator Father and Redeemer Son, it can be said to have told the monumental lie. Where Murdoch's critique is most relentless, moreover, is in its attack on what the character Hilary Burde in *A Word Child* calls Christianity's denial of causation and death, its "fairy-tale of constructive suffering":

> When I was a child I believed that Christ died for my sins. Only of course because he was God he didn't really die. That was magic all right. He suffered and then somehow everything was made well. And nothing can be more consoling than that, to think that suffering can blot out sin, can really erase it completely, and there is no death at the end of it all. Not only that, but there is no damage done on the way either, since every little thing can be changed and *washed*, everything can be saved, what a marvellous myth. . . .
> (WC 291)

One should normally be wary of ascribing a character's attitude to the author, and yet this indictment of Christianity's "magic," its denial of death, can be found throughout Murdoch's fiction as well as in her nonfictional writing. There is only a difference in tone between Hilary Burde's denunciation of the "marvellous myth" and Murdoch's essay, "The Sovereignty of Good Over Other Concepts" (1967): "To buy back evil by suffering in the embrace of good: what could be more satisfying, or as the romantic might say, more thrilling? Indeed the central image of Christianity lends itself to just this illegitimate transformation" (SG 82).

Hardly less culpable than religion in the matter of false consolation, however, is the realm of art. For here as well the primary menace to integrity is the "cosy dreaming ego," working its own magical redemption by imposing form upon contingent experience and thereby transforming it into a bogus construct of "significance." Murdoch's most sustained indictment of the magic of art, its "fantastic doctoring of the real for consumption by the private ego," is to be found in the latter pages of her study of Plato's aesthetics, *The Fire and the Sun: Why Plato Banished the Artists* (FS 79). But it is writ large throughout her work, philosophical and fictional alike — this exposure of the way the artist habitually brings closure to his or her representation of a life which is, in truth, radically open, flowing, incapable of any resolution or finality save for the ultimate one of death. The great temptation of art is always to succumb to the blandishments of fantasy, to present us with meaningful suffering, beautiful pain, the happy ending, the resolution of conflict. It is the temptation, in short, to portray reality tricked up and faked out.

Nonetheless, despite her contention that we are by nature self-seeking, and inhabit a universe which we are continually trying to transform into the fulfillment of our wishes, be it by religion or art or any number of other tactics, Murdoch's central interest lies in the possibility of self-transcendence, a breaking out of the dream of solipcism into the cold light of external, shared reality. There is the chance, in other words, that we can break through the prison of egocentricity to discover suddenly the existence of other people and their entirely independent claims. Once the self-enclosure of fantasy has been loosened, there is the possibility that the fat relentless ego can learn to pay *attention.* This crucial term, borrowed from Simone Weil, points to a concept foundational to Murdoch's moral as well as aesthetic vision. In her lexicon it signifies nothing less than the beginning and end of wisdom, this ability to cast a just and loving eye on another individual reality, to patiently confront the particulars of its case without grasping referral back to oneself, to open up to something else for no other reason, perhaps, than because it is irrefutably, nonnegotiably there.

As to the provenance of such grace, Murdoch has nothing to say. It is, to recall Wallace Stevens' poem "Sunday Morning," "unsponsored, free" — a gift received but not given. In the final analysis, it may result from some confrontation with human mortality, as when Murdoch writes, "The acceptance of death is an acceptance of our own nothingness which is an automatic spur to our concern with what is not ourselves" (SG 103). But Murdoch's fascination with the phenomenon of changed consciousness is not limited to realizations quite so grand or so ultimate, and examples of the simple ways it can occur are scattered throughout her essays, offering us crystals of what we find elaborately developed in her fiction. A mother-in-law, realizing her own biases, decides to take a second look, more just and loving, at her son's new wife. A person forgets her maelstrom of private hurts and preoccupations when through a study window she suddenly catches sight of a kestrel poised in mid-air. A student of Russian loses himself in the learning of a language utterly foreign to him, something which his consciousness cannot "take over, swallow up, deny, or make unreal." (SG 89) A man falls in love and discovers, as it were for the first time, another person who is as rich, strange, and unfathomable as himself.

The difficulty in each of these cases is to keep one's attention fixed in order that one may not fall back into self-absorption and fantasy and control, distortions of vision to which romantic love is especially inclined. But the still small truth about attention is that with modesty and resolve it can become not only a "habit of being," but a powerful source of moral discernment and action. However occasional, transitory, or partial success may be in this endeavor — and here we must remember that Murdoch is deeply pessimistic about the outcome — ordinary people are nonetheless capable of this kind of goodness, this attempt "to pierce the veil of selfishness and see the world as it really is" (SG 93). To attempt this at all runs so contrary to our nature that any motion in its direction must be seen as something of a miracle, an extraordinary moment of breakthrough in which the careful looking at another, however imperfect the effort, joins us both to the world and to the ideal of a Goodness that forever eludes our grasp: "a distant transcendent perfection, a source of uncontaminated energy, a source of *new* and quite undreamt-of virtue" (SG 101). Such a goal may seem remote to the student absorbed in his Russian verbs or the lady held fast by the sight of a hovering kestrel. But however dimly perceived it may be, for Murdoch this painful reorientation of the self outward, toward a perfection of goodness we can never attain or fully know, generates the only light in an aimless unwitting universe and the only real transcendence we can hope for.

There are two things which become strikingly clear in even a cursory examination of a Murdochian "conversion," this coming to oneself which occurs, paradoxically, when one admits the reality of something outside oneself. The first is the degree to which she transforms theological concepts and vocabulary in order to conduct her own philosophical discourse. In her hands dogma becomes myth, and myth a source of metaphors for exploring our unadorned human experience, our evenings that are always "evenings without angels," to recall once again a Stevens poem. And so she speaks of the practice of attention as a non-dogmatic prayer, translates sin, grace, and salvation into entirely humanistic terms, and in one essay, "On 'God'

and 'Good,' " expounds her Supreme Concept by systematically emptying a definition of God of all suggestions of divinity. Lacking any other language of transcendence, she takes and purifies the one inherited from Christianity (and to a lesser degree from Buddhism), aware of the temptation to fake up the Good in God's image and lend it His "consoling and encouraging role." Nonetheless, even with this danger of falsifying her own enterprise, Murdoch's demythologization offers a resonant vocabulary to express what she has no other words for: the depth of our experience and the discovery of otherness. In this way, she would argue, it is once again possible to return Christianity to the realm of the believable.[2]

In addition to this extensive process of translation, the second thing to notice in Murdoch's notion of transformed consciousness is the crucial role assigned to art as the great mediator of this nonreligious self-transcendence. Despite her Platonist suspicion of its magic, of the ease with which the imagination degenerates into "fantasy-consolation" and therefore into a betrayal of the truth, Murdoch believes that great art stands to offer us major access to the experience of unselfing described above. In Shakespeare and Tolstoy, Velasquez and Titian, we learn something about a proper reverence for humanity, about how "real things can be looked at and loved without being seized and used, without being appropriated into the greedy organism of the self" (SG 65). We learn, in fact, how reality can be seen truly, in all its contingency, absurdity and pain, so that beauty, rather than making life bearable, instead makes it inescapable.

Murdoch's particular heroes are the great novelists of the nineteenth century (George Eliot, Jane Austen, but most particularly Tolstoy) who, like Shakespeare, are able to give the reader an unforgettable experience of persons who are "substantial, impenetrable, individual, indefinable, and valuable," persons who are seen against the richly detailed background of a world both physically and socially dense.[3] This ability to create character, to give the reader an experience of what George Eliot called "an equivalent centre of self from which the shadows fall with a difference," is to offer that reader an experience of the sublime: the awesome apprehension that other people exist.[4] To be sure, characters are only aesthetic creations, and to attend to them is an infinitely easier proposition than to pay attention to another person. But for Murdoch the powerful experience of great art can quite possibly offer an initiation, a first step in a longer, far more complicated journey away from the canvas or off the page, into the real world upon which true art is always in attendance.

Given the incarnational thrust of this aesthetic, with its connection between the value of persons and transcendent notions of Value itself, it is not surprising that Murdoch should identify the work of the imagination as a *religious* undertaking. Both true art and true religion oppose fantasy in their struggle to see the "other"; both try to reformulate for each generation the metaphysical background against which we live out our lives. And so, adapting Tolstoy's ideas about the religious dimension of art, she appropriates a demythologized Christian vocabulary to describe the role that a work like *King Lear* can play in a person's life. Attending to the death of Cordelia, for instance, can be a kind of prayer, serving for many people as "the easiest available spiritual exercise," as a substitute for religious meditation, as "an analogy to the concept of a sacrament," as the means by which we realize "that there is more than this" (SG 65, 69). In these ways Shakespeare can occupy that middle ground between morality and mysticism once occupied by the Church, mediating between one's experience of the world and one's transcendence of its ordinary limitations and blinders. This is not to say that *King Lear* will escape misperception or false application, being like all art "defenceless against its clients" (FS 86); nor does it mean that an appreciation of it will necessarily lead to an amendment of life. There are no guarantees here, any more than there are with the Gospel. Nonetheless, as Murdoch says in her eloquent argument against Plato, art

> provides a stirring image of a pure transcendent value, a steady visible enduring higher good, and perhaps provides for many people in an unreligious age without prayer or sacraments, their clearest *experience* of something grasped as separate and precious and beneficial and held quietly and unpossessively in the attention. Good art which we love can seem holy and attending to it can be like praying. . . . Good art . . . provides work for the spirit.
>
> (FS 76-7)

The most powerful demonstration of this theory about the religious function of art in the life of non-religious persons is to be found in Murdoch's 1958 novel, *The Bell.* Most of the action in the book takes place in a small lay community associated with an enclosed convent of Anglican nuns and among Christians who are more or less disastrously trying to live some kind of "regulated" life outside the monastic walls. Into their midst comes a hopelessly muddled young woman, Dora Greenfield, who is totally out of place in this rather hothouse atmosphere of pious endeavor. Dora is not herself a Christian, having painlessly lost the vague religion of her childhood when she discovered that she could say the Lord's Prayer quickly, but not slowly. Her presence at Imber Court has to do with rejoining her estranged husband, Paul Greenfield, who has temporarily attached himself to the community while studying medieval manuscripts at the neighboring abbey. When tensions on all fronts seem to reach a breaking point, Dora impulsively flees back to London and into the arms of her lover, Noel Spens, who blames her frantic state on the atmosphere of guilt and self-abasement that for him characterize all Christian groups. Indeed, he is the voice of what Murdoch has elsewhere identified as the Ordinary Language Man, opposing the neurotic "rubbish" of religion with his own cool rationality: " 'They may be nice,' said Noel, 'but they're thoroughly misguided. No good comes in the end of untrue beliefs. There is no God and there is no judgement, except the judgement that each one of us makes for himself, and what that is is a private affair.' " His assurance fails to bring her comfort, however, and so with his words ringing in her ears — "Don't forget! No God!" — she takes refuge from the overheated chaos of her life in London's National Gallery. Walking through the "eternal springtime of airconditioned rooms," through galleries which she has visited many times before, Dora pauses briefly before a succession of paintings until Gainsborough's portrait of his two daughters holds her fixed:

> Here was something which her conscious could not wretchedly devour, and by making it part of her fantasy make it worthless. . . . The pictures were something outside herself, which spoke to her kindly and yet in sovereign tones, something superior and good whose presence destroyed the dreary trance-like solipsism of her earlier mood. When the world had seemed to be subjective it had seemed to be without interest or value. But now there was something else in it after all.
>
> . . . She felt that she had had a revelation. She looked at the radiant, sombre, tender, powerful canvas of Gainsborough and felt a sudden desire to go down on her knees before it, embracing it, shedding tears.
>
> . . . She gave a last look at the painting, still smiling, as one might smile in a temple, favoured, encouraged,

> and loved. Then she turned and began to leave the building.
>
> (B 203-4)

The narrator tells us that Dora drew no explicit moral from this extraordinary moment, but it is clear that we are meant to linger over its significance. We are meant to see, moreover, that great art provides access to the ineffable mystery which the Church once held in custody but which it holds no longer, at least for the increasing number of people like Dora Greenfield. What Murdoch does in this scene is take a renowned palace of art and show it to be, in fact, a temple, a holy shrine in which the worshipful observer encounters the "other" without knowing fully what has hit her. It is the human perfection of the Gainsborough double portrait that arrests Dora, with its studious, living presentation of two girls, "their garments shimmering, their eyes serious and dark, round full buds, like yet unlike." Faced by those faces, she finds something to challenge her "dreary trance-like solipsism" with the vital force of its own reality. The painting is "sombre, tender, powerful"; it offers a mystery that she feels, at a depth of consciousness quite beyond the reach of intellect, to be an unveiling of the real, a *revelation.* Given its impact on her, as in a kind of mystical ecstasy she longs to "go down on her knees before it, embracing it, shedding tears," we are led to see it as offering something like an experience of the *mysterium tremendum,* of a nameless holiness that defies definition, but which nonetheless transforms the one who has glimpsed it.

While Dora's intense veneration of the painting conjures up images of traditional Catholic devotion, Murdoch does not want us to understand the Gainsborough portrait as a revelation of God. Instead, through the painter's prayerful attention to his subjects, through his waiting upon their reality, the susceptible observer is launched on an experience of the Good: the realization that other things, other people, exist. By focusing our concern on the viewer of the painting, moreover, Murdoch gives us a portrait in prose of someone who is in a state of secular grace, illumined and enlarged by what she has seen — which may also be the experience of the reader through his or her absorption in this very scene. This is to suggest that Dora's encounter with art may show not only how a painting can provide the unbeliever with "work for the spirit," but also, by extension, how Murdoch's own fiction is working toward this same end. She has given the godless reader a godless character with whom to identify and from whom to learn, a woman who leaves the National Gallery as the reader may also close this novel, "still smiling, as one might smile in a temple, favoured, encouraged, and loved."

A passage such as this one from *The Bell* would seem to warrant identifying Murdoch with a type of contemporary novelist she has called "mystical," within whose ranks she includes Graham Greene, Patrick White, Saul Bellow, Muriel Spark, and William Golding, though not herself. In her view, these are all writers who are trying to express religious consciousness apart from the traditional trappings of religion — and indeed, if we include Murdoch in their number, without its theistic "content" as well. For such a novelist there is no conventional God, no Church, no social support or protective institutions, no easy connection morality, no consoling spiritual world. Instead we find an effort to invent meaningful religious imagery and discourse that is able to signify the importance of human reality within an otherwise indifferent cosmos. The idea of grace which one finds in the "mystical" novel is a growth in understanding which brings about some degree of obedience to the Good, usually without heroism or charm. Its characteristic virtue is humility or self-diminishment, and the dangers which it must hold fast against, the reintroduction of the "fatherly figure of God behind a façade of fantastical imagery or sentimental adventures in cosy masochism" (EM 174). With this caveat in mind, it is easy to imagine her no doubt withering assessment of Waugh's *Brideshead Revisited* as an example of everything to be avoided in this kind of fiction.

Murdoch's own attempts at the "mystical" novel, with its search for religious imagery "in an otherwise empty situation," seem to me to involve her in two broad creative tasks. The first is the evocation of a world which truthfully embodies reality as the author perceives it to be: a world in which the utter chanciness of human existence, together with the absolute full stop of death, form a kind of bedrock out of which everything else is carved. Contingency is for her the ground of all being, and therefore in some real sense is the great subject of her fiction. Secondly, it is against this "metaphysical background" that Murdoch wants to portray a multitude of vividly believable characters, as arresting to her readers as are Gainsborough's daughters to Dora Greenfield: characters mysterious and dense and valuable in their sheer humanity, and perhaps most poignantly so in a universe which has nothing to do with or for them. Such characters, seen against such a background, constitute what Murdoch speaks of as "the juxtaposition, almost an identification, of pointlessness and value" (SG 87); it is for her the hallmark of the greatest art.

The heart of this fiction is a person's enlargement of concern, his or her growth in attentive understanding, by which that person learns, against every natural odd, "to see the place of necessity in human life, what must be endured, what makes and breaks . . . so as to contemplate the real world (usually veiled by anxiety and fantasy) including what is terrible and absurd" (FS 80). This learning inevitably involves some purgation of the "fat relentless ego," but without what Murdoch speaks of as Christianity's "machinery of guilt and repentance," its often perverse enclosure of the self inside its own suffering.[5] Finally, the choice of the Good which this stark diminishment entails will always be seen as the choice of a goodness *for nothing*; a goodness that is without reward and without God, whose pursuit is what gives life whatever value it has.

The contrast with Flannery O'Connor could not be more striking, for if like her Murdoch impells her characters toward a face-to-face encounter with reality — and often brutally shatters their defenses and illusions in the process — the vision which they come to see, darkly and in enigma, is the mystery of another person. This is for her the vision of the Good hovering on the far side of her characters' experience: not God, but the human face divinely glimpsed in its "absurd irreducible uniqueness."[6] For models of such moments of breakthrough it is not to any contemporary practitioner of the "mystical" novel that she turns, but rather to Shakespeare and the Russian novelists, despite the vast differences between the metaphysical background of their works and that of the contemporary post-Christian writer. "Virtue standing out gratuitously, aimlessly, unplaced by religion or society, surprising us as it so often does in real life: the gentleness of Patroclus in the middle of a ruthless war, the truthfulness of Cordelia in a flattering court, Alyosha telling his father not to be afraid of hell" (EM 182).

This is where she aims, at an ideal of "lovingkindness" enacted between one person and another in a world where God is hidden, or absent, or dead. The effort of her fiction, therefore, is at once to conjure up this godless universe and to explore the possibilities of what we might call saintliness within it. But if this double intention constitutes an underlying program within Murdoch's many novels, contributing as much as anything else to one's sense of *déjà vu* in passing from one book to another, the fact remains that the texts themselves complicate and challenge their own premises, contravening what I have identified above as Murdoch's orthodoxy with the heretical possibility of a religious reading.

In *The Bell*, for instance, Murdoch juxtaposes Dora Greenfield and her rapturous experience in the National Gallery with Michael Meade, the leader of the Imber Court community and a character utterly different from her in temperament, history, and religious sensibility. Rather than a would-be artist, as Dora is, he is a would-be priest, and it seems clear that at least on one level Murdoch is exploring through their contrast the difference between a nonreligious transcendence of reality on the one hand and the failure of a traditional Christian life on the other. Given what we know about Murdoch's thought on these matters, it would seem likely for her to privilege Dora's "way" and dispose of Michael Meade's with the dispatch of the character Noel Spens: "No good comes in the end from untrue beliefs." To be sure, Murdoch does subject Imber Court to close scrutiny, as we see the added confusion that religion brings to sexuality, guilt, and power. But the novel does not treat the Christian aspirations of the community, let alone the hidden life of the abbey, as unworthy of respect. Meade's spirituality is presented not only with the loving objectivity Murdoch has so often enjoined on others, but also with an enormous sensitivity to the psychology of a believer. Knowing her theory, one can see the dangers implicit in his particular faith, but the fact that it is shown to be distorted by fantasy, rather than being fantasy itself, enables the reader to take that religion seriously, however problematic or esoteric it may seem to the Dora Greenfields reading Murdoch's novel. This tolerance is reinforced by Murdoch's brief portrayals of Mother Clare, the abbess of the convent, whose Christian counsel to Meade, if ignored by him, is nonetheless resonantly Good advice: "Remember that all our failures are ultimately failures of love. Imperfect love must not be condemned and rejected, but made perfect. The way is always forward, never back" (B 253).

Running parallel to the abbess's words throughout the novel are a string of allusions to Dame Julian's *Shewings of Divine Love:* "That which is impossible to thee is not impossible to me. I shall save my word in all things and I shall make all things well." The end of *The Bell* would seem to belie the truth of this Christian claim: one character is dead, another gone mad, and the lay community shattered in the wake of events. At the center of these several disasters is Michael Meade, who emerges from the wreckage in the company of Dora to find his own faith "broken at a single blow":

> He thought of religion as something far away, something into which he had never really penetrated at all. He vaguely remembered that he had had emotions, experiences, hopes; but real faith in God was something utterly remote from all that. He understood that at last, and felt, almost coldly, the remoteness. The pattern which he had seen in his life existed only in his own romantic imagination. At the human level there was no pattern. 'For as the heavens are higher than the earth, so are my ways higher than your ways, and my thoughts than your thoughts.' And as he felt, bitterly, the grimness of these words, he put it to himself: there is a God, but I do not believe in Him.
>
> (B 334)

As one might well expect, Murdoch writes as astutely about the loss of religious faith as she does about what it means to be a believer. But the narrator's presentation of

Meade's thought here asks us to ponder what exactly it is that has been lost. The passage makes a very clear distinction between the spiritual consolations that Meade's religion had once nourished — emotions, experiences, hopes, and above all a sense of purposeful pattern in his life — and *real* faith in God. The contrast seems to be between true faith and false, between a romantic consoling notion of God and a transcendent deity unutterably higher than human ways or thoughts, whose will cannot be secured on the human level. Meade approaches this distant divinity with the bitterness of a lover betrayed: "There is a God, but I do not believe in Him." And yet what the narrator leaves us with is the possibility that the breakdown of this man's religious framework may become a breakthrough into a larger, more mysterious, less self-oriented concept of God, one which may at first chill with its remoteness, but which corresponds rather closely to Murdoch's own idea of the Good.

The text, therefore, poses a number of interpretive questions. Is this the soul's dark night in which fantasies die on the brink of real faith in God? May this be, in fact, a religious experience of the most profound kind, such as Christ Himself may have known in the face of death, an experience of the absence of God? Or do we have instead Murdoch's painful stripping away of the illusions of religion, so that if there is a God one must realize that there is absolutely no way to live in terms of Him as in a personal relationship? With extraordinary deftness the author does not tip the scale in any direction. Quite the contrary, she seems deliberately to suggest a surprising equivalence (though not an identity) between Meade's religious desolation and Dora's Gainsborough ecstasy. In both cases an emptying of self frees the individual from the "anxious avaricious tentacles of the self" (SG 103); in both an act of attention marks the liberation.

For Meade this occurs within the context of the Eucharist, attendance at which remains the only formal vestige of his earlier practice:

> The Mass remained not consoling, not uplifting, but in some way factual. It contained for him no assurance that all would be made well that was not well. It simply existed as a kind of pure reality separate from the weaving of his own thoughts. He attended it almost as a spectator, and remembered with surprise the time when he thought that one day he would celebrate the Mass himself, and how it had seemed to him on that day he would die of joy. That day would never come, and those emotions were old and dead. Yet whoever celebrated it, the Mass existed and Michael existed beside it.
>
> (B 335-6)

The tone of this account is entirely different from the one used to describe Dora's experience, but there is nonetheless the same emphasis on facticity, on the discovery of a reality unentangled by the mind's weaving self-reflections. Meade no longer knows the uplift of the sacrament, or its old reassurances; it has ceased to be the stage on which to imagine himself, vested at the altar and dying of joy. There is, in fact, no joy here at all, but only the quiet observance of one who is now "almost a spectator." And yet if the magic of the Mass is gone, Meade is left with the sharpness of its focus: a point of reference outside himself that will not capitulate to his ego; a point by which to gain, perhaps, that "selfless respect for reality" which is for Murdoch the great virtue of humility.

In Dora we find the cup running over and in Michael Meade the pain of existing without consolation. In both we find an encounter with otherness that represents a step in the direction of the Good, however small or faltering it may be. Whatever personal reservations Murdoch may have about the Christian religion or the existence of God, the novel itself does not throw suspicion on the faith of the abbey or on the validity of the Mass as an experience of the real; it even hints that Meade's discovery of his own existence *beside* the sacrament may be precisely the discovery he needs to take him closer to reality and the route to a more genuine Christianity than his former faith had ever allowed him to penetrate. This latter scenario is not given by the text, which tells us only that Meade has found a teaching job in Norwich; it is but one possibility in his completely open future. What the novel does seem to suggest, however, is that Dora's experience in the Gallery and Meade's in the abbey chapel, for all their apparent differences, are both approaches to a mystery that if beyond naming or attainment — higher than the heavens, indeed — can nonetheless be pursued through a variety of means, even within the very traditional framework of the convent itself. In the final paragraph of the novel the abbey bell rings as if from another world, unintelligible to Dora, icily remote from Michael Meade, but in fact from another world in which to struggle toward "a distant transcendent perfection, a source of uncontaminated energy, a source of *new* and quite undreamt-of virtue" (SG 101).

Murdoch's critics have by and large been reluctant to deal seriously with her ambiguous religious propensities. The best of them, Elizabeth Dipple, has proved an exception to that rule with her sustained appreciation for the major paradox of Murdoch's work: "It is rather odd for a contemporary novelist who is not a servant of orthodoxy to have as a fundamental part of her style such a presentation of religious attention and love, especially when the main underlying ideas acknowledge contemporary society's loss of the workable religious concepts that once united it."[7] Others have been less charitable, such as the irate *New York Times* reviewer of *Nuns and Soldiers* who accuses Murdoch outright of being a "neo-Christian apologist" in a novel which includes a vision of Christ that is impossible to dismiss as an hallucination.[8] The confusion on all sides is understandable. It is difficult to know what to do with an author whose ideas on the nonexistence of God and the waning of religion are well known, but who nonetheless works increasingly within a religious framework, who writes about the full range of Christian experience with such extraordinary insight and sympathy, and who makes her most complete exemplar of the Good — Brendan Craddock in the novel *Henry and Cato* — a brilliant Roman Catholic priest. His presentation of the Christian *via negativa* is at the same time Murdoch's most eloquent articulation of her own philosophy: "The point is, one will never get to the end of it, never get to the bottom of it, never, never, never. And that never, never, never is what you must take for your hope and your shield and your most glorious promise. Everything we concoct about God is an illusion" (HC 374).

About her own religious position there can be little doubt. "I am not a Christian," Murdoch has said in interview after interview. There seems to me no reason to confuse her respect for Christianity as a "spiritual guide and inspiration", or for Christ as the "Buddha of the West" ("an image of spirituality, a teacher, and a centre of spiritual power"), with Christian belief itself.[9] What is in question, however, is the presence of religion in her fiction. And it is here that we find the crux of the matter, for in using Christianity as extensively as she has, and for whatever divergent end, she has run the risk of being used by it, of opening the eyes of her reader to those divine mysteries which it has been her stated business to humanize, demythologize, or dispel. What we may well have in Murdoch, therefore, is not a Christian *malgré lui,* but a novelist whose work communicates with great power the very vision it would translate and transform.

Perhaps the most telling way to explore this phenomenon is in a novel that answers more clearly to Murdoch's description of the contemporary world than the overtly religious contexts of *The Bell* or *Henry and Cato,* a novel where none of the characters has any religion to lose and the tide of faith seems at a permanent ebb. A case in point is her 1975 novel, *A Word Child.* Entirely narrated by the protagonist Hilary Burde, the book presents itself as a kind of unfinished memoir: the story of one man's coming to himself. For all the symmetrical intricacies of its plot, the novel ends with a sense of ambiguous openness — the "pierced" quality that Murdoch has argued to be a characteristic of the best fiction, where "a sort of wind blows through it and there are holes in it and the meaning of it partly seeps away into life."[10] Because of this mysterious indeterminacy, the reader is subtly forced into his or her own determinations as to what has really happened and what may still occur, quite independently of whatever the narrator-protagonist makes of his own situation. This makes possible the polyvalence I want to discuss further on.

Hilary Burde is himself the "word child" of the title, whose precocious genius for learning languages provided his way out of a childhood of misery and deprivation: "An ability to write fluent correct Latin prose began to offer me an escape from (perhaps literally) the prison house, began in time to show me vistas headier and more glorious than I had every dreamed of. *Amo, amas, amat* was my open sesame." The schoolboy's first conjugation of the Latin verb "to love" culminates in an Oxford career in linguistics and in an affair with the wife of his colleague, Gunnar Jopling, an affair which ends in the woman's death as a result of a car crash for which Hilary in his headlong selfishness is responsible. All this past history is filled in through an extended flashback. The action of the novel itself begins twenty years after Anne Jopling's death, as we see firsthand, through the filter of Hilary's own consciousness, the extent to which he has allowed guilt, resentment, and self-pity to warp not only his life, but also that of his sister and alter ego, Crystal. For after leaving Oxford in a self-enclosed disgrace, Hilary buries himself in a mindless civil service job and in an ironclad routine of nightly dinners and appointments (from which Crystal is largely excluded), a calendar of rigidly immovable feasts designed to protect him from thought, feeling, and the possibility of change. As more than one character observes, he is a "word child" who has turned his gift for language into a kind of autism, resolutely refusing to communicate with anyone except on his own tyrannical terms. It is a life of arrogant self-recrimination, a self-imposed torture to which Crystal has been forced by love to bear witness, though at the total expense of her own freedom and life: "She just had to be always available in a place fixed and controlled by me. I had to know, at any moment, where she was."

Into the midst of this underground existence, however, there falls the bombshell of the past. Gunnar Jopling arrives on the scene, newly remarried to a Lady Kitty and as chief of the government office for which Hilary works. With her elaborate encouragement, Hilary falls in love with the second Mrs. Jopling as he did with the first, though now in a heightened euphoria of romance and drama that turns this self-loathing narcissist into a knight with a quest, a suppliant before a goddess. Although Hilary is warned by a number of others about what might come of this dalliance, he cannot break the hold of its magic upon him, even though the miraculous reconciliation with Gunnar that finally occurs is brought about not through the machinations of Lady Kitty, but rather by the quiet intervention of Crystal. But then, when the facts of their situation become unavoidable even to one bewitched — as he wisely tells Kitty, "from here another step and we are destroyed" — the horror of the past returns to haunt him with uncanny devastation. Bizarrely, absurdly, unintentionally, accidentally, Hilary brings about Kitty's death and in so doing more than doubles his own nightmare. The brief remainder of the novel shows his attempts to live in a world now empty of the consolations within which he had once fortified himself, such as his routine of "days," his placing on Crystal's shoulders the weight of every woe, his sense of control. It is a world where sheer accident reigns supreme, in which grief itself must be given up lest it once more distort his life with its chronic self-involvement. As he comes to reflect in the book's great recognition scene, there was "simply a loose end which guilt would twist, and the only salve, indeed the only duty, was to recognize the impossible, standing as it were at attention before some end-point of human endeavour" (383).

This severe, almost Aeschylean wisdom represents a new limit to Hilary's old sense of "authorship." It is an acceptance of the fact that the past cannot be undone or made bearable, let alone changed through despite; there is indeed an endpoint to human endeavor. And yet the novel does not conclude in any kind of tragic resolution, but rather with the "loose ends" more characteristic of comedy: the possibility of new life, of the continuing story, of a chance to be happy even in a world of horror and pain. We see this comic aspect in the "Christmas Day" epilogue to this December novel, just after Crystal's wedding to her longtime suitor Arthur Fisch. At that time Hilary is confronted by two revelations from his erstwhile fiancée, Thomasina Uhlmeister, who has pursued him throughout the novel. She confesses that she once wrote a letter to Gunnar Jopling exposing Hilary's love for Kitty, a letter for which she now asks his forgiveness though in complete ignorance of its consequences: "Unknowing Tommy had brought about the encounter which killed Kitty and married Crystal and brought double-intensified eternal damnation into my life and Gunnar's." To her request for pardon he answers, "I expect so. As I said, time will show." But with regard to her second revelation, her renewed plans to make him her husband, he is considerably more ambiguous. The novel ends with the following exchange:

> We were standing at the corner of Kensington Church Street. It was beginning to snow quite fast now. The bells of St. Mary Abbots were ringing Christmas in with wild cascades of joy. Other churches nearby had taken up the chime. The Christ child, at any rate, had managed to get himself born.
> 'Happy Christmas, Tommy.'
> 'I'm going to marry you, Hilary.'
> 'Are you, Thomas?'
> 'Yes, I'm going to marry you.'
> 'Are you, Thomasina?'

As Hilary declines the name of this would-be wife (Tommy, Thomas, Thomasina), *A Word Child* closes with a question that may be teasing, contentious, rhetorical, or dismissive. It also brings about one of Murdoch's more tantalizingly open closures, so that we are left uncertain as to what Hilary will do with either of the matters Tommy has thrown at him. But as the novel has gradually developed the equation that forgiving another person means, in fact, to be forgiven oneself, so this comical figure of Fate seems to have placed in his hands the opportunity to forgive her, and in that act to break out of the compulsive circles of recrimination and repetition in which he has run his entire life. Murdoch pulls back from the happy ending, or perhaps from any notion of ending whatsoever, and in doing so she forces us to take into the silence that follows her speech the options which the novel has offered: to forgive and thereby be forgiven, or not.

The veteran reader of Murdoch's fiction finds in *A Word Child* a familiar story told afresh, for what she has given in the particular circumstances of Hilary's life is another exploration of moral awakening, of the way the "fat relentless ego" meets the hard realities of necessity and chance. In that confrontation he not only comes to see himself a great deal more modestly, but also learns to bow his head before the impenetrable mystery of other persons. However rudimentary its development, however inconclusive its beginnings, this is also the story of a conversion to the Good, toward which we see Hilary struggle upstream, as it were, against the raging current of his own "penitence, remorse, resentment, violence, and hate." Again, we do not know what will come of the changes wrought in him by the novel's events, but that there *has been* significant change goes without question. The man whom we see in the end — mourning the death of a friend, setting his sister free without letting her know it — is someone who has broken through his own ranks, perhaps capable at last of "forgiving [himself], forgiving them all."

What I am identifying here as the thematic substructure of *A Word Child* offers few surprises. More disconcerting, however, is the predominance of a Christian frame of reference in a novel where only one extremely minor character ("Skinker") is a Christian. By predominance, I mean more than the fact the book opens on an unspecified Thursday in Advent and closes as bells peal in Christmas morning; more also than the choice of T.S. Eliot's parish church (St. Stephen's, Gloucester Road), replete with its iconography of incarnation and crucifixion, as the scene of Hilary's major coming to himself. What I am referring to is the continuous use of a theological vocabulary, of words like sin, grace, reconciliation, redemption, and salvation. There is the obsessive reference to the "sentimental old lie" of Christianity, the appropriation of its myth to describe the identity of persons in their relation to one another, and all of this by a cast of characters who say, over and over again, that they do not believe in God.

The easiest way to understand this phenomenon is to see it as Murdoch's attempt to suggest the liminal position in which many people find themselves today. They are caught between Christianity's former cultural presence and its present waning or, as it often seems to be expressed in this novel, between the fantasized religion of childhood and adult unbelief. The situation is a poignant one; characters talk about God as nonexistent, or as having imperceptibly vanished from the scene, and yet the language of God-talk nonetheless seems to be the only one they have to convey the depths of their experience, their longing for some kind of transcendence, the feelings they cannot yet put into any other words or find new symbols to express. Thus one character, wanting to give Hilary something, presents him with a cheap metal cross and chain, even though he is more sure about the existence of flying saucers than about God. Tommy, in her desire to relieve Hilary of his sense of guilt and pain, at one point offers herself as Jesus Christ ("after all — they say — we can be") and on another occasion extends him forgiveness "on behalf of God." Crystal longs throughout the novel to see the Christ child's crêche in Regent Street, partly (one suspects) out of nostalgia, but also out of a more profound wish that the old story might be true: "I wish we still believed in Jesus Christ and that he could wash away our sins."

If these wistful traces of a religion largely lost account for the faint aura of Christianity in *A Word Child,* it is to the protagonist-narrator that we must turn to understand its central importance. Raised in an orphanage permeated by an "overly-lit, overly-simple, covertly threatening" evangelicalism, Hilary emerges from his childhood with an enormous sense of personal guilt (hideously corroborated by the death of Anne Jopling) and a bitter loathing for the religious "machinery" that was supposed to take it all away. Although at the beginning of his narration he describes himself as having "no religion and no substitute for it," it is immediately clear that he but slenderly knows himself in this regard, for in rejecting Christ's "fairytale of constructive suffering" he has actually constructed a salvific myth of his own in which the significant women of his life become redeemers, either by their innocent affliction (Crystal) or through their transforming "grace" (Anne Jopling and, to an even greater degree, Lady Kitty). Thus as the novel unfolds we see the extent to which Hilary's revulsion from Christianity actually masks a perverse appropriation of it: he martyrs himelf in an attempt to expiate his own sins and turns his sister into both Virgin Mother and sacrificial lamb. This is nowhere more clear than in his response to Crystal's longing for a Jesus Christ who could wash away our sins: "Well, since there's no Jesus it'll have to be your love that saves me, Crystal, so don't stop praying, will you?"

Through Hilary Murdoch seems to be pointing out the predicament of people who are burdened by guilt, but who have no God to forgive them, no sacrament of reconciliation to help separate out the "tiny grain of penitence" from the grosser elements of the human muddle. Through him she also exposes the great danger of religious myth when it is projected onto other persons, especially when the mythmaker stands totally outside the disciplines of religion and lacks the guidance of a Mother Clare or a Brendan Craddock — people who know how easily religious notions can degenerate and destroy. But whereas she will occasionally use Hilary's rejection of Christianity to voice her own objections to it, as we have seen above, *A Word Child* draws our attention primarily to the pernicious quality of *debased* religious fantasies rather than to any frontal criticism of Christianity itself. In fact it is Hilary's particular brand of atheism, with its concommitant exaltation of self as "author" and expiator, that prevents him from knowing and doing the Good, from the possibilities of forgiving and being forgiven.

What we may speak of as Murdoch's own religious vision breaks the surface of the narrative through two characters, both of whom seem strangely to embody St. Paul's description of the faithful as "not many wise according to the flesh, not many mighty, not many noble" (I Cor. 1.26). The most developed of these humble apostles of the Good is Arthur Fisch, who uses his Tuesday evenings with Hilary to try to get him to make peace with Gunnar Jopling; that is, to seize "the chance to do some good here" by discounting the possibility of reconciliation. Hilary finds this "guff about forgiveness" unacceptable because it seems to imply a belief in God; in fact, he accuses Arthur of talking "like a bloody theologian." To a certain degree he is correct, for although Arthur is not a Christian, his reply to Hilary is a faltering articulation of Murdoch's own demythologized faith:

> 'All right, I don't believe in God either. But I think that one should stick to simplicity and truth. There may be no God, but there's decency and — and there's truth and trying to stay there, I mean to stay in it, in its sort of light, trying to do a good thing and to hold onto whatever you know to be good even if it seems stupid when you come to do it. You could help

> yourself and Crystal, you could help [Gunnar], but it can only be done by holding onto the good thing and believing in it and holding on, it can only be done sort of — simply — without dignity or — drama — or — magic —' (290)

This relinquishing of "magic" is for Murdoch one of the signs of spiritual greatness, and shines here through Arthur's pleas for a simple "holding onto the good thing" even as it lies behind Brendan Craddock's decision to put aside the formal study of theology at the end of *Henry and Cato*. What it would require of Hilary, however, is a stepping out of the way, a diminishment of self that would entail a loss of drama, dignity, and the peculiar power of the one who suffers. Most difficult of all, it would mean thinking of Gunnar as separate from himself and thereby allow a space to lie open between them. But because all this sounds to Hilary like "that illusion, that simple old fiction. . . the Jesus Christ story," he rejects it out of hand, telling Arthur, the non-Christian believer in a "faithful sort of — good will," that he has no intention whatsoever of travelling to the "Precious Blood Mission Hall" where Arthur's words seem to beckon him. Instead he moves straight on to disaster.

Something very different happens to Gunnar Jopling in the course of his conversation with the novel's other exemplar of the Good, Crystal Burde. Through her he reaches the point of being able to let go of the hatred that had disfigured his life since Anne's death, to lay the ghosts to rest and to say to Hilary, "[There] is so much accident in all things. I suppose in the end all things must be forgiven." When a dumbstruck Hilary tries to find out how his "victim" could say such things, could even ask Hilary's forgiveness for the past, Gunnar explains how Crystal had comforted him the previous evening with her simple affection, her absurd fish fingers dinner, and a quote from the

Bible: "Whatsoever things are true, whatsoever things are honest, whatsoever things are just—." Philippians 4.8 is the sort of text a schoolgirl might well remember, a bit of generic wisdom to be taken out on occasions that are otherwise too deep for tears. And yet we are quite clearly meant to take what it says seriously here, for it is Crystal's recital of St. Paul that enables Gunnar to "think on these things" and find in truth, honesty, and justice the antidote to his self-enclosed misery of the last twenty years. Within the novel, however, it is Hilary who actually completes the verse for Gunnar, the terrible irony of this bit of verbal recall being his refusal to understand what the words mean or to interpret them as having any significance for him. It is precisely his inability to turn his attention to "whatsoever is of good report," and to hold onto the Good even when it seems stupid to do so, that keeps him inside his prisonhouse of self. As he did with Arthur's pleas for a reconciliation, so he abruptly dismisses Crystal and her quotation: "She's full of Biblical lore. It's all that she knows." And yet once again we see that his rejection of what he disdains as religious is, in fact, a refusal of the one kind of redemption which *A Word Child* offers.

It comes as an enormous surprise, therefore, that when catastrophe accomplishes the breakthrough that Good words could not effect, Hilary's great moment of awakening should occur within the very traditional setting of an Anglo-Catholic parish long associated with T.S. Eliot and replete with golden reredos and "little baffled lights flickering in the dark." To be sure, the unbelievers in Murdoch's fiction often seek refuge in the deserted quiet of such places, looking for "something" where it used to be found. But Hilary's choice of St. Stephen's is singularly striking given the antipathy toward Christianity which he has shown throughout the length of his narration. Once furious with Arthur for sounding like a "bloody theologian," he now enters a church finally to make peace with the universe and there to express many of the familiar Murdochian verities. The reader is led to expect, in other words, that this is far more than the dusty museum of some fiction no longer supreme; that it is, at the very least, as vital and holy a temple as the National Gallery, for instance. I am not suggesting that the change of consciousness which Hilary reveals there is presented as a Christian one, for it is quite clearly a secular equivalent of conversion and in its great emphasis on the sheer accident in things squarely at odds with Christian belief. Nonetheless, Murdoch seems in this episode to be making positive use of an ecclesiastical setting, as if the moral distance Hilary has travelled in the course of his narrative is being measured by his having chosen to come here. It is as if the mystery to which St. Stephen's bears silent witness is somehow to be associated with his new apprehension of the Good, so that the church becomes a place to forgive and be forgiven, however one understands the meaning of that exchange.

The ambiguity that Murdoch's positive use of St. Stephen's occasions intensifies at the very end of the episode, as Hilary focuses his attention on the church's iconography and allows it to gather up all the thoughts and feelings that have preoccupied him in his darkened pew.

> At one end of the aisle under a tasselled canopy the Christ child was leaning from his mother's arms to bless the world. At the other end he hung dead, cut off in his young manhood for me and for my sins. There was also, I saw, a memorial tablet which asked me to pray for the repose of the soul of Thomas Stearnes Eliot. How is it now with you, old friend, the intolerable wrestle with words and meanings being over? Alas, I could not pray for your soul. . . . But I could feel a lively gratitude for words, even for words whose sense I could scarcely understand. If all time is

> eternally present all time is unredeemable. What might have been is an abstraction, remaining a perpetual possibility only in a world of speculation.
>
> (383-4)

There is no talk here about false consolation or sentimental old lies; indeed, Hilary has come so far as to be able to speak of Christ "having died for me and for my sins" not only without rage, but with a kind of genuine reverence. Even if he does not believe that such a redemptive death is possible — even if he is simply speaking the formulaic language of the place in which he only momentarily stands — this Christian imagery of loving self-sacrifice seems to facilitate the secular religious experience that Murdoch's characters are occasionally graced to know. For what do we find at the close of this episode but Hilary caught in an act of worship, attending to the reality of others, grateful for words of poetry and humble enough to acknowledge he can as yet but scarcely understand them, "praying" the words of Eliot's poem "Burnt Norton" and discovering in that other man's wrestle with words and meanings some new wisdom by which to live.

But it is precisely in this intertextual moment, as Hilary's language loses itself in recollection of T.S. Eliot, that we find Murdoch's own work opening up to another possibility of grace than the one we know as her own. This is not immediately apparent. Abstracted from their larger poetic context, Hilary's paraphrase of the opening of the *Four Quartets* seems to confirm the stoic resignation he has come to since Kitty's death: his acceptance that the past cannot be "folded up and in the twinkling of an eye everything [be] changed and made beautiful and good." Such an attitude would also echo Murdoch's own view of our "real situation," of "the world as it is." But of course it must be remembered that the words with which Hilary closes the episode are only the beginning of Eliot's poem. If one reads further in it, the text moves the reader in an entirely different direction, for after the poem's initial assertion that "all time is unredeemable" (an assertion made in the conditional mood of "if") there is an altogether different claim based on the intersection of the timeless with time:

> The hint half guessed, the gift half
> understood, is Incarnation.
> Here the impossible union
> Of spheres of existence is actual,
> Here the past and future
> Are conquered, and reconciled. . . .
>
> ("Dry Salvages" V)

For Eliot, the incarnate "here" where time is redeemed is none other than the Christ before whose images Hilary stands at attention but in whom he does not believe, the Word of God toward whom the whole of the *Quartets* makes its move "into another intensity/ For a further union, a deeper communion/ Through the dark cold and the empty desolation," to quote the lines from "East Coker" that are inscribed on Eliot's memorial in the real St. Stephen's Church. Although the significance of one text within another is always difficult to determine, it is unlikely that anyone who recognizes the *Quartets* here will fail to recall that poem's hopeful ending when Hilary paraphrases its rather hopeless beginning. This does not mean that Eliot's Christian vision preempts Hilary's experience of the dark cold and the empty desolation, nor that the "word child" in him has embarked upon a journey to some deeper communion with a God he does not yet believe in. But what we do see in Murdoch's handling of this crucial moment in the novel is the subtle way she poises religious alternatives, voicing a denial of Christ's redemption and evoking an unspoken affirmation. Thus the reader is left in a "world of speculation" indeed, caught between a notion of time unredeemed and the hope of its being conquered and reconciled, that is, between the beliefs of Iris Murdoch and those of T.S. Eliot.

The ambiguity which I am suggesting in this particular episode also characterizes the novel when it is reviewed as a whole. For while the arbitrary and accidental nature of things is constantly maintained by one character or another, what we actually find there is something more open to interpretation: a world of magical symmetries, uncanny coincidence, signs and wonders. Supposedly random events occur in significant patterns, in running reference to a liturgical season of expectation, and in what can readily appear to be a fullness of time. It may well be fantasy to see in human life any kind of sense or unity beyond what we ourselves create, but in Murdoch-land it is easy to doubt this, easy to consider quite the contrary possibility that there is some purpose in the universe working out its inscrutable intentions. For may there not be some purpose that keeps Hilary in its grip until he can barricade himself against life no longer, but must come up above ground, stand in the painful light of day, and either choose to forgive and be forgiven or once again burrow back into the guilt-ridden cave from which he has been, as it were, called out?

There is a tension, in other words, between what we have come to know as Murdoch's beliefs about life and her evocation of an unnamed mystery inexplicably welling up and fomenting the world of her fiction. With this mystery comes a sense of radically open possibility that is supposed to convince us that the universe itself is "aimless, chancy, and huge" (SG 100). But what is to prevent the reader from taking the extraordinary course of these events not as fortuitous but as providential, as the action of divine grace that tears Hilary out of his solipsistic cocoon and thrusts him into the same midnight in which "the Christ child, at any rate, had managed to get himself born"? What is to prevent us from identifying the new life available to Hilary at the very end of the novel with the Christ event, or to keep us from entertaining the notion that in giving Hilary the chance to forgive and be forgiven Thomasina Uhlmeister may well have been Jesus Christ for him?

By juxtaposing the life of her "word child" with Christ, the Word of God, Murdoch has created a puzzle for the reader which *she* refuses to solve. Officially, of course, the divine redeemer has nothing to do with anything real, being at most a *façon à parler,* a great human exemplar of the Good. And so presumably it is also with the theological frame of reference that shapes this particular novel as it does so many others. God is introduced as an absence, a fantasy to be exorcized, a subject for redefinition in the manner of Arthur Fisch or Crystal Burde, a kind of Wittgensteinian language game in need of renovation. And yet, I would argue, the presence of the Christian story throughout *A Word Child* allows us to consider whether the unnamed mystery portrayed there might not be, in fact, divine grace. It allows us to ask, in the context of St. Stephen's Church and Eliot's *Four Quartets,* whether the consolation which Christ offers is necessarily sentimental and false. It enables us to entertain the possibility that God speaks His own word in the muddled *amo amas amat* of human experience, perhaps not disclosing His speech or His activity but nonetheless giving us the chance to say something utterly new — something like, "I forgive you" — and then to be transformed by that speech act.

In the end *A Word Child* leaves us free to choose an understanding of its events, even as we are left free to understand our own lives and to make some kind of sense out of them. To be sure, no less than O'Connor and Percy, Murdoch structures her narrative along the lines of her own religious angle of vision. Like Percy in particular, she peoples it with characters who more or less openly speak in the voice one comes to recognize as the author's own; she has her message-bearers, too. As with both these Christian writers, she will use crisis to shatter illusion, life and limb, thereby giving her protagonists the opportunity to become someone new, to see reality in a different and often more painful light. But far more than O'Connor or Percy, it is the peculiar gift of Iris Murdoch to leave us at the end of a novel asking questions. They are not, as with O'Connor, about what she means, nor, as with Percy, about the viability of what her protagonist has chosen. Rather, they are questions about the text itself which rapidly become questions about one's own reading of it. In other words, Murdoch leaves us with the self-revealing burden of our own act of interpretation. The experience of her fiction forces a heightened consciousness of how life is to be understood, either in relation to God or without Him. By confronting the reader with an unnamed mystery on the one hand, and with a set of Christian "names" on the other, the dots are there to be connected in different patterns that lead to altogether different pictures. The text remains as ambiguous as life itself. Thus, what Murdoch's fiction offers, I think, is the strange possibility of a religious discovery that the author has not made for herself, an encounter with the Word she has no intention to speak, but which is perhaps all the more powerful for the author's final silence before the options she has arrayed. Compared with O'Connor and Percy, this is indirect communication in the extreme. But the language of grace which it articulates seems to me no less eloquent for its indirection, for the freedom in which the reader is finally left alone with a choice before a mystery that will not easily give over its burden.

NOTES

Notes to Chapter 1

1. *The Habit of Being,* pp. 90, 126, 227. Hereafter cited in the text as L.

2. "A House of Theory," *Partisan Review* 26 (winter 1959): 17-31, p. 28.

3. *The Parables of Jesus* (New York: Charles Scribner's Sons, 1963), p. 21. My understanding of the parables has also been enriched by two works of John Dominic Crossan, *In Parables: The Challenge of the Historical Jesus* (New York: Harper & Row, 1973) and *The Dark Interval: Toward a Theology of Story* (Niles, Ill.: Argus Communications, 1975), as well as by Dan O. Via, *The Parables* (Philadelphia: Fortress Press, 1967) and Amos N. Wilder, *The Language of the Gospel* (New York: Harper & Row, 1964).

4. Cited by Eta Linnemann, *Jesus of the Parables* (New York: Harper & Row, 1966).

5. Via, p. 188.

Notes to Chapter 2

1. L 85. An excellent book-length study of the problematic relationship between O'Connor, her work, and the unbelieving reader can be found in Carol Scloss's *Flannery O'Connor's Dark Comedies: The Limits of Inference* (Baton Rouge: Louisiana State University Press, 1980).

2. The fullest account by O'Connor of her own faith is to be found in her letters and most especially in her correspondence with "A." For her more public statement, see two essays in *Mystery and Manners,* "Novelist and Believer" and "Catholic Novelists and Their Readers."

3. Joyce Carol Oates, "The Visionary Art of Flannery O'Connor," in *Women Writers of the Short Story*, ed. Heather McClave (Englewood Cliffs, N.J.: Prentice-Hall, Inc., 1980): 150-62, p. 154.

4. M 44. Readers interested in the connection between O'Connor's fiction and her region should see Robert Coles, *Flannery O'Connor's South* (Baton Rouge: Louisiana State University Press, 1980) and *Flannery O'Connor's Georgia*, photographs and text by Barbara McKenzie (Athens, Ga.: University of Georgia Press, 1980).

5. M 112. One wonders if O'Connor was influenced in her concept of divine grace as a kind of lethal assault by a passage in a work she knew well, Teilhard de Chardin's *The Divine Milieu* (New York: Harper & Brothers, 1960): "God must, in some way or other, make room for Himself, hollowing us out and emptying us, if he is finally to penetrate into us. And in order to assimilate us in Him, He must break the molecules of our being so as to re-cast and re-model us. The function of death is to provide the necessary entrance into our inmost selves" (p. 61). For Teilhard's importance to O'Connor, see Sr. Kathleen Feeley, *Flannery O'Connor: Voice of the Peacock* (New Brunswick, N.J.: Rutgers University Press 1972), pp. 116-20.

6. For a fuller treatment of this story, see my essay, "Problems of Overstatement in Religious Fiction and Criticism," *Renascence* 33 (autumn 1980): 36-46.

7. See M 168.

8. M 111-12. O'Connor also interpreted the story in a few letters, namely to John Hawkes (L 389-90) and "To a Professor of English" (L 436-37).

9. The Carol Scloss book mentioned above is amazingly free of enthrallment to O'Connor's intentions for her work, as are Martha Stephens, *The Question of Flannery O'Connor* (Baton Rouge: Louisiana State University Press, 1973) and Clara Claiborne Park, "Crippled Laughter: Toward Understanding Flannery O'Connor," *The American Scholar* 51 (spring 1982): 249-57.

Notes to Chapter 3

1. Robert Coles, *Walker Percy, An American Search* (Boston: Little, Brown and Company, 1978) gives a good introduction to Percy's life in relation to his work.

2. For Percy's full treatment of this subject, see his essay, "The Loss of the Creature," MB 46-63.

3. Coles, p. 193.

4. See Coles, especially chapter 1. Also Martin Luschei, *The Sovereign Wayfarer: Walker Percy's Diagnosis of Malaise* (Baton Rouge: Louisiana State University Press, 1972), chapter 2, and Bradley R. Dewey, "Walker Percy Talks About Kierkegaard: An Annotated Interview," *Journal of Religion* 54 (1974): 273-98. A critic who does pay attention to the connection between Percy and O'Connor, however briefly, is Susan S. Kissel, "Voices in the Wilderness: the Prophets of O'Connor, Percy and Powers," in Jac Tharpe's edited collection, *Walker Percy: Art and Ethics* (Jackson: University Press of Mississippi, 1980), pp. 91-8.

5. Erich Auerbach makes his famous distinction between narrative foreground and narrative background in a comparison of Homer with the author of Genesis 22.

See *Mimesis: The Representation of Reality in Western Literature,* trans. Willard R. Trask (Princeton: Princeton University Press, 1968), chapter 1.

6. The contrast here is with O'Connor's notion of a "realism of distances" (M 44, 179), where visible events are always envisaged in the light of their extensions into eternity.

7. John Romano, *New York Times Book Review,* June 28, 1980.

8. See MB 108-9. Cf. "The Man on the Train," MB 83-100.

9. LG 300. Compare MB 115.

10. Kierkegaard's essay, "Of the Difference Between a Genius and an Apostle" was instrumental in Percy's conversion to Christianity. It is published with "The Present Age," trans. Alexander Dru (New York: Harper & Row, 1962).

11. R.W.B. Lewis, *The Picaresque Saint: Representative Figures in Contemporary Fiction* (Philadelphia and New York: J.B. Lippincott Company, 1959).

Notes to Chapter 4

1. EM 177.

2. Murdoch's fullest statement on this matter was made in a formal address to a group of academics at the University of Caen, published in *Rencontres avec Iris Murdoch* (Caen: L'Université de Caen, 1978), pp. 16-7: "It is equally interesting that after a period of irreligion or relative atheism there have been signs of a kind of perceptible religious renewal in certain changes in theology. I am ignorant of the extent to which this

has been felt in France, but I think that in England one is experiencing a demythologization (to use this fashionable term) of theology which recognizes that many things normally or originally taken as dogmas must now be considered as myths. In this there is something which might have a profound impact on the future which, for the ordinary person, might return religion to the realm of the believable. T.S. Eliot said that Christianity has always adapted itself in order to be believable. Thus, if one defines art in religious terms, I believe its vocabulary is not outmoded and that one might even be able to establish a connection between the work of theology and that of art in their actual form." (Translation mine.)

3. AD 20. Murdoch's criticism of Sartre's fiction, for instance, is largely a criticism of his failure to create characters who live in real relationship to other persons and to society. In a chapter entitled "The Impossibility of Incarnation" she writes the following: "Sartre's lovers are out of the world, their struggle is not an incarnate struggle. There is no suggestion in Sartre's account that love is connected to action and day to day living; that it is other than a battle between two hypnotists in a closed room" (p. 96).

4. For Murdoch's notion of the sublime as the recognition of other persons, see "The Sublime and the Good," *The Chicago Review*, XIII, no. 3 (autumn 1959), 42-55 and "The Sublime and the Beautiful Revisited," *Yale Review* 49 (December 1960): 247-71.

5. A good example of this purgation of the "fat relentless ego" is the kind of "clean" suffering which Michael Meade undergoes at the end of *The Bell*: "The annihilating sense of a total guilt gave way to a more reflective and discriminating remembrance. It was indeed as

if there was very little of him left now. He need not have feared to grow, to thrive upon disaster. He was diminished. Reflection, which justifies, which fabricates hopes, could not do so now for him," p. 330.

6. See Bledyard's discussion of portraiture in *The Sandcastle* (1957) for Murdoch on the sublimity of another person's face seen in and of itself: "But who can look reverently enough upon another human face? The true portrait-painter should be a saint — and saints have other things to do than paint portraits. Religious painters often understand this obscurely. Representations of Our Lord are usually not presented as if they were pictures of an individual. Pictures of Our Lord usually affect us by the majesty of the conception, and not by any particular expression or gesture. Where the picture is individualized, as in Caravaggio's rendering of Christ at Emmaus, we are shocked. We should be equally shocked at any representation of a human face," pp. 81-2.

7. Elizabeth Dipple, *Iris Murdoch: Work for the Spirit* (Chicago: University of Chicago Press, 1982), p. 95. Dipple's book is far and away the best, most complete, and up-to-date study of Murdoch. It also has an excellent bibliography of works by and about her.

8. George Stade, *New York Times Book Review*, January 4, 1981.

9. Michael O. Bellamy, "An Interview with Iris Murdoch," *Contemporary Literature* 18 (1977): 129-40, see p. 134; *Rencontres*, pp. 77-8.

10. Bellamy, p. 132.

Cowley Publications is a work of the Society of St. John the Evangelist, an Anglican community of priests and brothers dedicated to the Incarnation of the Word of God. Our publications, along with our work of preaching, spiritual direction, and hospitality form an important part of our mission as stated in the Rule of our founder: 'To be instrumental as far as God may permit in bringing others to be partakers of that same consecration to which God in his mercy calls us.' These publications extend from our call and our dedication to the whole of Christ's Church.

The Revd. M. Thomas Shaw, SSJE
The Revd. Russell Page, SSJE
Br. James Madden, SSJE